USMC PHANTOMS
in combat

by Lou Drend

illustrated by Lou Drendel

squadron/signal publications

ISBN 0-89747-235-7

If you have any photographs of the aircraft, armor, soldiers or ships of any nation, particularly wartime snapshots, why not share them with us and help make Squadron/Signal's books all the more interesting and complete in the future. Any photograph sent to us will be copied and the original returned. The donor will be fully credited for any photos used. Please send them to:

Squadron/Signal Publications, Inc.
1115 Crowley Drive.
Carrollton, TX 75011-5010.

Photo Credits

McDonnell Douglas
U.S. Marine Corps
U.S. Navy
Norman E. Taylor
George Cockle
Jack Hunt
Manny Simpson
Jack McEncroe
Mule Holmberg
Dave Fuller
Robert F. Dorr
Fred Harl
Dr. Joseph G. Handeman
Jerry Geer
Schinichi Ohtaki
Harry Gann

INTRODUCTION

Marines have been involved with the F-4 Phantom from its initial testing until its final phase-out from the active Naval Air Forces during the late 1980s, a period covering more than 30 years.

When it first entered service during the early 1960s, the Phantom was the hottest fighter in service and it broke every speed and time to climb record then in existence. The Marines did their share of record-breaking with the Phantom. LTCOL Thomas H. Miller set a 500 kilometer closed course speed record of 1,216.78 mph on 5 September 1960. The world absolute speed record was set on 22 November 1961 by LTCOL Robert B. Robinson in an F-4A (BuNo 142260). The speed runs were made at 45,000 feet, at an average speed of 1,606.3 mph, which equates to nearly Mach 2.6. Robinson's feat was a testament to both man and machine, since he was required to maintain altitude to within 100 feet during the twenty mile speed runs (two runs through the timing gates, in opposite directions, are required for an FAI certified speed record). LT William C. McGraw, Jr. set the 9,000 and 12,000 meter time to climb records on 1 March 1962 (61.62 seconds and 77.15 seconds, respectively.). These Project High Jump missions were flown at NAS Brunswick, Maine. The rate of climb achieved in these two missions exceeded 30,000 feet per minute!

The first Marine Corps Phantom squadrons were VMF(AW)-531, at Marine Corps Air Station (MCAS) Beaufort, South Carolina, under LTCOL Robert F. Foxworth, and VMF(AW)-314, at MCAS El Toro, California, under LTCOL Robert J. Barbour who had been the first Marine to fly the Phantom (BuNo 143388) in October of 1959 at NATC Patuxent River, Maryland. Both squadrons transitioned to the Phantom during the Spring of 1962. The 'AW' in the squadron designation indicated the squadron was an all weather fighter squadron. Later, it was more properly replaced with the VMFA designation, with the 'A' indicating attack, which is what the Marines intended to use their new fighter for anyway.

The third Marine squadron to receive the Phantom was VMFA-513, at MCAS El Toro, followed by VMFA-542. All four squadrons deployed to Atsugi, Japan, during 1963-65 to become part of Marine Air Group 11 (MAG-11). MAG-11 deployed to Danang, South Vietnam, during 1965. It was the beginning of an eight year commitment to the war zone, which finally ended when VMFA-232 left Nam Phong, Thailand, during September of 1973.

USMC squadrons which flew the Phantom in combat in Southeast Asia included:

VMFA-115 Silver Eagles	VMFA-122 Crusaders
VMFA-232 Red Devils	VMFA-314 Black Knights
VMFA-323 Death Rattlers	VMFA-333 Shamrocks
VMFA-334 Falcons	VMFA-531 Gray Ghosts
VMFA-542 Bengals	VMCJ-1

Other USMC Phantom squadrons were:

VMFAT-101 Sharpshooters	VMFA-112 Wolfpack
VMFAT-201	VMFA-212 Lancers
VMFA-235 Death Angels (flew the F-8 Crusader in SEA combat)	
VMFA-251 Thunderbolts	VMFA-312 Checkerboards
VMFA-351	VMFA-451 Warlords
VMFA-513 Flying Nightmares	VMCJ-2 Playboys
VMCJ-3	VMFP-3 Eyes of the Corps.

With the popularization of Tom Wolfe's classic, "The Right Stuff," the mystique of the fighter pilot was catapulted into the public eye. Although its main characters were astronauts, "The Right Stuff" went to the very core of what it takes to strap on a high performance, single-seat, yank and bank airplane. Literary fans and (to a much lesser degree) movie fans rediscovered military courage, idealized like it hadn't been since World War II. "The Right Stuff" created a market for books, television, and movies about fighter pilots, and the market was quickly filled.

LTCOL Thomas H. Miller broke the 500 km closed course speed record in an F4H-1 Phantom (BuNo 145311) on 5 September 1960. He set a new record of 1,216.78 mph. (U.S. Navy)

The F4H-1 Phantom and its Lockheed F-104 Starfighter chase plane made a low pass over McDonnell employees after its record-breaking flight. (U.S. Navy)

The original Phantoms were equipped with a McDonnell-designed ejection seat. When McDonnell test pilot Zeke Huelsbeck was killed attempting to eject from a disabled Phantom, the company switched to the Martin Baker Mk 5 seat. (U.S. Navy)

3

If "The Right Stuff" did it for astronauts and rocket pilots, "Top Gun" did it for Naval Aviators and "Call to Glory" did it for USAF pilots; what popular book/film has done it for the Marines? If you can forget about "Black Sheep Squadron," which claimed to recount the life and times of Pappy Boyington's VMF-214 (a randy bunch of misfits commanded by the epitome of a hard-drinking, brawling, hell-for-leather Marine) then my candidate would be "The Great Santini."

Where "Black Sheep Squadron" was somewhat frivolous, and often downright silly, "The Great Santini" was a serious examination of the life and times of a Marine Corps fighter pilot. "The Great Santini" was the true story of a Marine Corps fighter squadron commander. He was stubborn, arbitrary, and absolutely dedicated to the Corps. He epitomized the fighter pilot in every sense of the genre, being unconventional, competitive, dedicated and courageous. His courage and selflessness in his final moment of truth also epitomize what ultimate service to country is all about. Ultimate service to your country is where fact and the fictional glorification of the fighter pilot often diverge. Flying fighters is dangerous business, in war or peace, and the stakes are as high as they can get.

An anonymous author penned the following tribute to fighter pilots:

Say what you will about him: arrogant, cocky, boisterous, and a fun-loving fool to boot — he has earned his place in the sun. Across the span of fifty years he has given this country some of its proudest moments and most cherished military traditions. But fame is short-lived and the world little remembers. Almost forgotten are the 1,400 fighter pilots who stood alone against the might of Hitler's Germany during the dark summer of 1940 — and in the words of Sir Winston Churchill gave England — Its finest hour. Gone from the hardstands at Duxford are the P-51's with their checkerboard noses, that terrorized the finest fighter squadrons the Luftwaffe had. Dimly remembered is the 4th

Fighter Group that gave Americans some of their few proud moments in the skies over Korea. How fresh in recall are the Air Commandos, who valiantly struck the VC with their aging A-1 Skyraiders in the rain-and-blood-soaked valley called A Shau? And how long will be remembered the F-105 Thuds over Route Package Six and the flak-filled skies above Hanoi? So here's a "nickle on the grass" to you, my friend, for your spirit, enthusiasm, sacrifice, and courage, but most of all, to your friendship. Yours is a dying breed and when you are gone — the world will be a lesser place.

Fighter pilots are a breed apart and so are Marines. Put the two together and you get more arrogance, enthusiasm, boisterousness, and...right stuff...per square foot than almost anywhere else. It is an elite of the elite (I think the same thing would happen if you gave the 82nd Airborne its own jet fighter squadrons). Marines are unconventional and you are about to find out how that translates to combat in the F-4 Phantom.

In "USMC Phantoms in combat", you will read the personal combat narratives of six Marine F-4 pilots. Their war was the Vietnam War, an altogether unsatisfactory period of U.S. military history. Unsatisfactory because, in the final analysis, the American public was unwilling to accept John F. Kennedy's challenge to "go anywhere and pay any price in the defense of liberty." President Kennedy chose Southeast Asia as the testing ground for his world vision of America as the defender of democracy. Unfortunately, both he and his successor lacked the political or moral courage to follow through on this choice. JFK saw the loss of Vietnam as the road to defeat in the 1964 elections and did not want to let the American electorate think that he was giving up on Southeast Asia. His attempts to control events in Vietnam led to the assasination of one of the two strong Vietnamese leaders. When President Diem was killed in a Kennedy-approved coup, the only strong Vietnamese leader left was Ho Chi Minh.

LBJ inherited a policy which required total commitment to be successful. He also inherited advisors who saw Vietnam as a political liability — not the battleground of democracy. Lyndon Johnson's choice of civilian advisors did not enhance that thinking. His Vietnam policies were founded on the premise that the enemy would settle for something less than total victory and that they would be willing to make a deal. That is a dangerous assumption if your

An F4H-1 (BuNo 149460k) of VMF(AW)-531 over MCAS Cherry Point, North Carolina during 1962. The Gray Ghosts of VMF(AW)-531 were **either the first or second Marine Corps squadron to receive the Phantom, depending upon whose version (theirs or VMFA-314's) of history you believe. (USMC via Jack Hunt)**

enemy has the means to destroy you. It is a stupid assumption if you have the means to destroy your enemy, while he has little more than the ability to harass you.

The American Military was never defeated during the Vietnam War. Neither was it ever allowed to be totally victorious. The rules of engagement, as defined in Washington, denied the military the complete military victory which was always possible. Every Marine aviator in the 1st Marine Aircraft Wing was issued a card with the Rules of Engagement. This card was small enough (2 1/2 inches by 3 inches when folded in half) to be carried in the sleeve pocket of a flight suit. The rules read:

GENERAL RULES OF ENGAGEMENT
FOR THE FIRST MARINE AIRCRAFT WING IN RVN

1. Visually identify target or target marker (except TPQ-10, MSQ-77, or DIANE system).
2. Know position of friendly forces.
3. Radio contact if working with FAC/TACA.
4. Wingmen and helicopter gunners or crew are only authorized to fire on command of the flight leader or pilot in command.
5. IN EMERGENCY SITUATION with no qualified means of control, the following may designate a target:
    a. Ground unit commanders or U.S. advisors engaged with hostiles (must possess radio capabilities).
    b. Army target identifying pilot (TIP).
    c. Pilot of aircraft or helicopter who is taking fire that presents an immediate threat to himself and/or members of the crew AND CAN:
    (1) Positively identify the source.
    (2) Positively orient a strike.

A Marine Corps F-4B Phantom II about to plug into the refueling receptacle from a KC-130F tanker over Southeast Asia. The KC-130 was the primary tanker for the Marine Phantom squadrons. (USMC)

SPECIFIC RULES OF ENGAGEMENT FOR STRIKE
PILOTS AND N.F.O.

1. Must have positive radio contact with designated control agency (airborne or ground).
2. Must have visual contact with target or target marker (except TPQ-10, MSQ-77, DIANE).
3. Know position of friendlies.
4. Defend selves against ground fire providing:
    a. Source can be visually identified.
    b. Strike can be positively oriented against the source.
    c. Fire of such intensity that counter action is necessary.

VMFA-531 manned the Key West hot pad during the Cuban Missile Crisis and was one of the first Marine Corps squadrons to see combat in Southeast Asia. The F4H designation for the Phantom had been changed to F-4B by this time. (USMC via Fuller)

The KC-130F Hercules tanker is capable of carrying 3,600 gallons of fuel in fuselage tanks and can refuel two aircraft simultaneously from drogues deployed from wing tanks. The KC-130F was able to transfer up to 31,000 pounds of fuel while flying at a speed of 355 mph and an altitude of 25,000 feet. (USMC)

Marine squadrons flying the Pacific (known as a Trans-Pac) refueled from KC-130F tankers between California and Hawaii. Normally two F-4s would refuel at a time and when they finished the next two would refuel until the entire squadron had been topped off. (USMC)

VMFA-531 F-4B Phantoms shared the Danang Air Base flight line with U.S. Air Force North American F-100 Super Sabres during April of 1965. For most of the war, Danang was a joint USMC/USAF base. (USMC)

5. Strike at night only with flares, unless under control of TPQ-10, MSQ-77 or DIANE system.

REMEMBER

1. When in doubt hold your fire!!
2. Know location of friendlies!
3. Minimize non-combatant casualties and civilian property damage!

Number one, above, is an accurate assessment of Washington's policy in Vietnam. The politicians were often in doubt and usually held their fire. Asking a pilot who is flying a jet fighter at speeds of 400 to 600 knots when he drops his bombs to minimize non-combatant casualties and civilian property damage is ridiculous. Quite often, the ground troops had a tough time sorting out the good guys from the bad guys, and the communists had no compunctions about hiding behind the civilian populace, or using their property for shelter.

It was abundantly clear to those who were doing the fighting that they could not win as long as these rules, or some form of them, remained in effect. In spite of this, the military soldiered on, trusting to the political wisdom of American civilian leadership. Their job was to do the best they could under the circumstances. They did that...and more. The stories of individual courage and sacrifice that come out of the Vietnam War are our only national solace from that period and Marine Corps Phantom pilots provided their share of those stories.

DAVE FULLER

VMFA-531 deployed to Danang, South Vietnam, from its base at Atsugi, Japan, with the first aircraft arriving on 10 April 1965. The aircraft would never again look as clean as they were upon arrival at Danang. (USMC)

Dave Fuller's military career spanned a period of twenty years and he retired at the ripe old age of 35! The fact that he was able to enlist in the Army when he was only fourteen and complete a four year hitch without anyone realizing his adolescent status was remarkable, especially since he had enlisted when everyone else was getting out of the service during the post-war draw-down of the armed forces which began during 1946.

Fuller re-enlisted in the Marine Corps during 1950, at the beginning of the Korean War. He served as a Marine infantryman and was decorated during his two combat tours. He returned from Korea as a Buck Sergeant with a hankering for something more from the Marines than the infantry offered. The word was circulating that the Marines were looking for volunteers to train as Airborne Intercept Officers (AIOs) for their fledgling fleet of F3D Skyknight all weather interceptors. Dave volunteered and was one of thirteen men accepted from the 300 volunteers that applied for the program. That was the beginning of his career as a professional AIO, Radar Intercept Officer (RIO) and Naval Flight Officer (NFO), a back-seater to the pilot community.

At the time when the Phantom II was still a McDonnell company project, in competition with the Vought F8U-3 Crusader for the next Navy fighter contract, Fuller decided that he would like to visit McDonnell Aircraft on his next leave. He wanted to find out as much as he could, first-hand, about this new fighter. He wrote McDonnell explaining who he was, and why he was interested. McDonnell wrote back extending an invitation to visit the factory when he got to St. Louis.

His reception at McDonnell Aircraft was pure VIP (Very Important Person). Mr. Mac himself welcomed Fuller, while other company high ranking brass waited in the reception area. McDonnell explained that getting the opinions of the guys who would fly his airplane operationally was sometimes much more important that anything the brass might have to say. Dave was given a complete tour of the factory and questioned at length about his job and how the airplane could be designed to facilitate the mission. He was impressed with just about everything he saw at McDonnell and left the factory hoping he would get the chance to fly in the Phantom II.

He served with VMFA-542, at MCAS El Toro, California, until they turned in their Skyknights (and AIOs) for the single seat F4D Skyray. Fuller went to GCA (Ground Controlled Approach) school and was commissioned as a Warrant Officer in 1961. During 1962, he was assigned to VMFA-531, one of the first Marine squadrons to get the new F4H Phantom II. They began transition training in July of 1962 and, as an East Coast squadron, they were included in the

Florida build-up during the Cuban Missile Crisis in October of 1962. During that period, new pilots reporting into the squadron stood hot pad duty after only eleven hours experience in the aircraft. As Fuller says, "The hot pad really was hot at that time!" His combat experience was limited to a three month period during 1965, which came at the end of a one year Far East tour for VMFA-531. The events leading up to Vietnam were almost as exciting as those first combat missions. This is his story.

We were fortunate because we were very experienced in the Phantom before we went to Vietnam. I would guess that the average must have been about 500 hours per crew, so we really knew the airplane. Unfortunately, all of that time had been spent practicing the interceptor mission. When we got the word that we were going to Vietnam, we were told that we would be utilizing the Phantom in its "other" role...dropping bombs. A great deal of our experience in air-to-ground had been right at the beginning of our Phantom flying. After the Cuban Missile Crisis we were sent to NAS Key West to man the hot pad. We stood five minute alerts and actually did a lot of scrambles after off-course airliners. Since we were in an actual real-life air defense posture, we got all the spares and flying that we wanted.

VMFA-314 was the first Phantom squadron to transpac to Japan and we were the second. Our route was from Cherry Point to California, on to Hawaii, then island-hop to Japan. We were part of MAG-11 at MCAS Atsugi, Japan, and as things began heating up in Vietnam, we trained like we knew we would be going there. Our squadron stayed together, as a squadron, longer than any others that I know of...probably at least three years. In late 1964 we were sent to the Philippines to prepare for Vietnam. Many of our pilots had no air-to-ground experience and, with the exception of those of us who had come up through the enlisted ranks and seen air-to-ground from the ground, none of the RIOs had any bomb-dropping experience. There was a lot of head scratching as we tried to figure out what books to pull out for review and just how to go about getting proficient at dropping bombs.

There was a little island off the coast of NAS Cubi Point, Philippines, and we began using that as our target. At first, the island itself was used as the bulls-eye, and we counted it a successful mission if we hit the island. None of our airplanes were wired for dropping bombs and that created some very interesting situations. As I recall, all the intervalometers were wired backwards and you never quite knew what was going to happen

LTCOL William C. McGraw, Jr. was the commander of VMFA-531 when it moved from Atsugi to Danang. Marine KC-130s refueled the Phantoms enroute and the move was completed on 11 April. Their first combat missions were flown two days later, on 13 April 1965. (USMC)

when you hit the pickle button. We would roll in, hit the pickle, have nothing come off, pull off, then sit there wondering how to get rid of the ordnance. Some of the switchology was pretty arcane...stuff like, "pickle, reset, pickle, pickle, reset pickle." (I don't know if that is how it actually went, but you get the idea.) You can imagine how difficult that made the bomb runs. There you are, on the perch, trying to remember the exact switchology for dropping the bombs before you even considered the geometry of the bomb run.

In spite of the problems, we did have fun! A lot of the fun was off duty, and was sponsored by the Captain of one of the ships which had been involved in the Tonkin Gulf Incident. This particular officer had begun his career as a Marine Corps enlisted man and he never forgot his Marine roots. We met him at the Cubi Point Officer's Club and struck up an immediate friendship. It seemed like every other drink inspired the Marine Hymn. His ship was in port for a little over a week and we all but chased everyone else out of the club during that time, with our drinking and singing. All we had to do to earn a round of drinks from the Navy was to buzz his ship when we took off on the first mission of the day. The runway orientation at Cubi was such that a buzz job of a ship tied up in the harbor could be accomplished immediately after takeoff if you did a wingover after retracting gear and flaps. The first mission of the day was usually about 0600, and some of those nights in the club didn't end until 0100. Some of those wingovers were kind of exciting!

The late nights were tough on the early missions, but we preferred them anyway, since it got so hot during the day. It was not uncommon to see runway temperatures of 120 to 130 degrees in the afternoons. Generally, we flew three missions per day, and did them consecutively. After landing, we would taxi to the refueling pit, "hot" refuel and rearm, then take off on the next mission. If you were lucky, you were finished by noon. If you started at 1100, you usually suffered through some terrific heat and didn't finish until 1600. Those middle-of-the-day missions produced some interesting experiences too.

It was January of 1965 and we were flying as much as possible, trying to work up our proficiency at dropping bombs. We hadn't carried much of anything but missiles prior to this and our CO had instituted a policy of no-flap takeoffs to get us airborne faster in air defense scramble situations. That worked O.K. with the lighter air defense weapons loading (missiles and

Danang Air Base, South Vietnam was a large complex housing both Marine units and U.S. Air Force squadrons. The base was under the operational control of the Air Force. (USMC)

drop tanks) and in cooler temperatures, but when we started loading the airplanes with bombs and encountered some of those horrendous afternoon temperatures in the Philippines, it got real scary.

On one of those afternoons, we were the fourth or fifth airplane in the flight to take the runway. It was hot and we were heavily loaded. As we lifted off, it became apparent that we were in trouble. The airplane was flying, but it was not accelerating and it was not climbing. It just sat on the edge of a stall, 150 feet in the air, with about a 45 degree angle of attack, heading for the big mountain off the end of the runway. By this time, the pilot and I had flown together for a long time and we had our emergency procedures pretty well worked out. If he gave the word, I was prepared to eject. It became obvious that we had flown into a blind alley, and there was no way out at our weight and control configuration. This was before our ejection seats had 'zero zero' capability (which allows aircrews to eject at zero altitude and zero airspeed and survive.) We were well out of the ejection envelope, but, under the circumstances, it was still the best choice and when he gave me the word I pulled the seat handle.

We were practically right in front of the control tower at the time and, fortunately, this particular system worked perfectly, with the parachute opening a split-second before I hit the ground. It didn't kill me, but it did break my back and injure my tongue (I wasn't smart enough to think of anyplace but between my teeth to store my tongue before the ejection). Amazingly, the force of the ejection, combined with the loss of a few hundred pounds of weight, allowed the pilot to fly the airplane out of its "almost stalled" condition and he landed safely. It took me almost two months to get back on flight status, but the squadron still had not been sent to Vietnam, so I didn't miss much of anything. I did miss survival training, or "snake school" as we called it and some of my squadron mates accused me of deliberately breaking my back to avoid it, which gives you an idea of how much we enjoyed snake school. The squadron returned to Japan after snake school, leaving me behind to recuperate. I rejoined them in time to make the move to Vietnam.

We had been expecting to go the Vietnam for months. Alert had followed alert, always with the disappointment of a stand-down. Towards the latter part of March, we were on alert for a solid week with no result. On Friday afternoon we got the word to stand-down...go out and have a good time...which we never had trouble doing. As we straggled in early Saturday morning we were told that there was an 0800 briefing for the move to Vietnam — THAT DAY! We hardly had a chance to get excited though before they called it off again and dismissed us for the day. But before any of us could get to the front gate, we were recalled and told to grab whatever we could fit into the airplanes and report to operations for the briefing. We were going to Vietnam — NOW!

Twelve airplanes left for Danang that day, arriving in Vietnam during the afternoon. Three others had various small problems and these were assigned to the most experienced crews, who were told, "to get there anyway you can by Sunday afternoon." I was in one of those three crews and we managed to get to Danang on Sunday, using mutual support to overcome the various avionics problems of the three airplanes.

Robert McNamara was Secretary of Defense at that time and he was taking a lot of heat from the press because of a lack of ordnance. During early 1965 there was great popular support for the war and any shortage of weapons created great political pressures. He denied that there was an ordnance shortage, but we certainly did not have everything we were supposed to have. Our main mission was close air support for the Marines and about the only weapons we had in any numbers were 500 pound bombs and 5 inch Zuni air-to-ground rockets. The 500 pounders were not the greatest for precision close air support, so we tried to save the Zuni rockets for those missions. Later on we got napalm, but it was the old World War II type in large red tanks.

We never knew for sure whether it would even go off when we dropped it. According to the Air Force, you never bring ordnance back. They always figured it was too dangerous to land with live bombs, but if you don't have enough to begin with, you are reluctant to waste what you do have, so we usually brought back what we didn't drop.

Danang was a joint Marine and Air Force base and their tower operators would always ask us what those big red tanks were. In order to avoid arguments, we told them that they were fuel tanks. We were fortunate that we could scrounge whatever we needed to get the job done, but it was not easy at times. We had no bomb loader and you can imagine what it was like trying to load 500 pound bombs by hand. Naturally, we went across the field and "borrowed" one from the Air Force. When they found out where it went, they came and took it back. Then we went and "borrowed" another and finally managed to hang onto one long enough to get us through the tour.

The squadron Commanding Officer at the time, COL McGraw, and I flew the first combat mission for the squadron. It was a close air support mission, under the control of a Forward Air Controller (FAC) flying an O-1 Bird Dog. It was a pretty unremarkable way to begin a combat tour. The fact that we had no perimeter security around our compound was potentially more exciting than the missions. Because of my combat infantryman background, I was put in charge of security. That was a challenge because we had no individual weapons to speak of. We managed to trade various items to the ground Marines for some M14 rifles, some old machine guns, and a few hand grenades. We felt a little safer and fortunately, we never had to use them.

We settled into a routine of flying missions during the day, then coming back for a few beers at the club and a check of the perimeter security before calling it a night. One mission that sticks out in my mind was an unscheduled night mission. I had already flown two missions that day and was relaxing with my second or third beer when the word came down that one of the regularly scheduled crews had to cancel out and a replacement was needed. The mission was the closest thing to a milk run that we got. It was a radar bombing run. All we had to do was fly an assigned course, up around 30,000 feet, and pickle off our bombs on command from the ground radar station, which used radar offsets to figure the bomb release point. These were flown against area targets, where absolute precision was not a prerequisite. I volunteered to fly the mission, along with a pilot I was not normally assigned to (since it was so routine, we figured the couple of beers we had wouldn't impair our performance).

LTCOL Harry G. Robinson, Executive Officer of MAG-13 at Chu Lai, takes off on a close air support mission for Marine ground troops in contact with the enemy on 1 July 1967. The Phantom is loaded with Mk 82 low drag bombs and two wing tanks. (USMC)

When we got to the briefing, we discovered that the name of the game had been changed. The mission was now close air support, under flares dropped by "Spooky", the Air Force AC-47 gunship which was armed with three six-barreled 7.62MM miniguns, each capable of firing 6,000 rounds per minute. Spooky also carried flares, a big load of gas and was being used as a FAC for fighters, as well as providing some pretty awesome firepower on its own. Bombing under flares is a tough mission, which requires you to concentrate and react quickly to avoid losing control of the airplane. It is also a guaranteed vertigo-producer. This was the first time we had ever flown this mission, so we had no previous experience. In fact, we had never even been trained for this mission! And this was for real. The mission had been changed because there were troops in contact who desparately needed the support. We did get there and managed to repulse the attack, though we had a very interesting moment when we lost one engine in the middle of our final bomb run. Fortunately, we managed to get it re-lit and returned to Danang...where we really needed another beer!

Dave returned to MCAS El Toro, California, with the squadron after its brief three month tour in Vietnam. He was later transferred to VMFA-122 and helped get that squadron ready to go to Vietnam. He retired before they left and eventually started his own management company in Dallas, Texas, where he resides today.

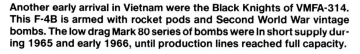

Another early arrival in Vietnam were the Black Knights of VMFA-314. This F-4B is armed with rocket pods and Second World War vintage bombs. The low drag Mark 80 series of bombs were in short supply during 1965 and early 1966, until production lines reached full capacity.

Loaded with bombs for a close air support mission, an F-4B of VMFA-314, flown by COL Norman W. Courley, commander of Marine Air Group 13 (MAG-13), flies wing on an A-4F Skyhawk flown by COL Rex A. Dessy, commander of MAG-12. (USMC)

MAJ E.R. Black was flying his 300th and final mission with VMFA-314 when a hydraulic failure prevented his port main landing gear leg from extending. The runway at Chu Lai was foamed and, after two attempts, Black landed safely. The F-4B sustained minor damage and was later repaired. (USMC)

Two Marine ground crewmen man a portable fuel pump at Chu Lai's fuel pit to refuel F-4Bs of Marine Air Group 13 (MAG-13/VMFA-314) after a mission on 11 August 1967. (USMC)

(Above) MAJs John Tyler (left) and Robert Miller of VMFA-314 took thirteen hits in their Phantom over North Vietnam on 19 March 1967. The biggest hole was from a shell that caused an engine fire. The fire went out after they shut down the engine, enabling them to make a safe landing at Danang. (USMC)

(Below) An F-4B (BuNo 151405) of VMFA-314 at Ubon Royal Thai Air Base, Thailand during 1968. As the war went on, Marine Corps Phantoms began to sprout the lumps and bumps of additional avionics and electronic counter measures equipment. (Al Piccirillo via Norm Taylor)

LTCOL DICK KINDSFATER

...reported in to VMFA-314 in October of 1968. The total bombing moratorium on North Vietnam had just gone into effect, so all of the US airpower was being concentrated on South Vietnam, Laos, and Cambodia. VMFA-314 was short of backseaters, so an NFO could pretty much write his own flying ticket. He could, in fact, spend his whole tour climbing in and out of airplanes. That is what Dick did, flying some 600 combat missions while accumulating over 725 combat hours. His airplane was never hit by hostile fire and none of his missions were so extraordinary that they stand out in his mind. But his experiences were many and varied. They provide further insight into how the air war was fought.

Over 90% of my missions were close air support of ground troops, with the balance being air combat patrols over Laos. During my tour, VMFA-314 lost three airplanes and two crews, while our sister squadron on the base, VMFA-115 averaged an airplane and crew each month. Practically all of the opposition in South Vietnam was from small arms with very few tracers, so we usually did not see them shooting at us. The FAC could see it and tell you about it, but the only time we saw the stuff they were shooting was when we went to Laos. In Laos we ran into fairly heavy concentrations of 37MM and 57MM anti-aircraft fire. Our tactic in Laos was to roll in high and fast, pickle at 9,000 feet, and pull out by 6,000 feet. That put us outside the effective range of most of the anti-aircraft fire, although I'm not too sure we were really effective, dropping from those altitudes.

Pilot technique had a lot to do with whether or not you got shot and everyone had their own ideas on how to avoid ground fire. In our squadron, we figured the best idea was to go as fast as you could around the target and to never remain straight and level for very long. We always had G on the airplane as we "jinked" to avoid possible ground fire. The fusing on most bombs limited your top speed, but we often pushed those limits and dropped most of our ordnance at 500 to 550 knots. We never had a problem with "dud" bombs at those airspeeds!

During my tour, I thought we were really kicking their butts. We flew anywhere we wanted, anytime we wanted, and they couldn't do a thing to stop us. I arrived in-country right after the battle of Khe Sanh, which was the North Vietnamese Army's big push against the Marines. We really decimated them and we never encountered much resistance from them after that. The Marines were involved in four major campaigns while I was there and, as far as I could tell, they were never hurting for air support in any of them.

The perspective you get flying missions is unique. I sometimes flew six or seven missions a day, in three different countries. You can't see much from the cockpit of an F-4 at 550 knots, a mile above the ground, so our impressions were generated from much of what the FAC told us. We would check in, get a target, roll in, pickle, pull off and wait for him to tell us what we had done. Now, that doesn't give you much of an idea of what the big picture is, but when you start going to the same places over and over again, you get a feeling for the flow of the action.

When I went through training, the primary duty of the F-4 backseater was defined as Radar Intercept Officer (RIO), which is an air-to-air mission. In Vietnam, there were very few missions where we actually performed that duty. We acted as a co-pilot without controls, reading checklists, keeping the pilot advised of bombsight settings for the various dive angles, cross winds, airspeeds, calling off the airspeed and altitude during bomb runs, and using that second set of eyes. Our radar was built for air combat, but when you got good with it, you could use it in a limited ground-mapping mode. Many times, that was the only Navaid you had. Over in Laos, for instance, the TACAN might start spinning and the Nav Computer wasn't very good, so the radar allowed you to cross-check your position. Very often, it was the difference between getting back to base or not under

"special VFR" conditions. (Author's note: "Special VFR" is a clearance issued to operate under visual flight rules when minimum ceiling and visibilities would otherwise dictate instrument flight rules.) If we lost our navigational radios, we were automatically operating VFR, whether we had VFR conditions or not. Special VFR was a clearance we issued ourselves, based on our judgement of whether or not we could see the ground and maintain separation from obstacles. The controllers didn't much like it, but the choices were often special VFR or eject from the airplane, since we didn't have enough gas to do much of anything else.

I always considered the weather to be a bigger danger than the enemy. During the monsoon season, the field was right at minimums (100 foot ceiling, half mile visibility) or lower just about all the time and we operated twenty-four hours a day. It rained all the time and the runway had a high crown, so you had to be lined up pretty good on landing. We usually took short field arrestments when it was that wet. Some of the big thrills in that environment were getting back to the field when everyone else did, low on gas, and be told you were number thirteen for the GCA (Ground Controlled Approach). Figuring fifteen minutes per airplane on the GCA, it didn't take long for guys to start declaring emergencies and trying to buck the line. That started a domino effect and pretty soon everyone had declared an emergency and the GCA was really squeezed. We tried to plan our fuel so that we had enough for a divert field. The first divert field was Danang, but since it had the same weather pattern as Chu Lai, you often had the same problems. We preferred to go to Phu Cat, the big USAF base to the south. Often their weather would be better than ours. When the weather really got bad, we had to plan our bingo fuel to go to Thailand, either Udorn or Korat. That really limited the mission time and, while we had KC-130 Hercules tankers, they weren't always there when you needed them. You never counted on them, because as soon as you did, they wouldn't be there. I would say that running out of gas was a bigger threat than enemy ground fire while I was there.

I left Chu Lai during 1969 and returned to the states, where I joined VMFA-531. I went through Top Gun and eventually got back to Southeast Asia with VMFA-115. The United States had left South Vietnam by that time and we were operating from Nam Phong, Thailand. Most people thought the war was over for the United States, but we were still flying combat missions during 1973 in support of the South Vietnamese Army and into Cambodia against the Khmer Rouge. By August of 1973 Congress shut off all funds for combat operations and we shut down at Nam Phong and flew the airplanes to Japan.

An ordnance maintenance man checks the electrical circuits on the launch rails before loading a pair of Zuni rockets into their tube launchers aboard an F-4B of VMFA-115, on 4 September 1968. The Zuni was the largest rocket used by the Marines in Vietnam. (USMC)

The Marines used this TD-4595 Darwood Tractor to tow Phantoms, like this F-4B of VFMA-122, around the flight line at Danang. (USMC)

A Sats weapon loader moves Mk 82 low drag bombs, already mounted on a Multiple Ejector Rack (MER), on the VMFA-122 flight line at Danang during 1968. (USMC)

A Marine Ordnanceman inserts the nose fuse into a 250 pound Snakeye bomb on the outboard wing station of a MAG-13 Phantom. Normally bombs were not carried on the outboard stations because it restricted the aircraft's maneuverability. (USMC)

This Ordnanceman is gently installing a nose fuse on a 250 pound bomb. The F-4 is loaded with a MER (six bombs) on the outboard station and a TER (three bombs) on the inboard station. (USMC)

The Sats weapons loader used by VMFA-122 at Danang greatly speeded up the rearming of Phantoms between missions. Without the loader the bombs would have had to be loaded on the MERs after they were attached to the aircraft, a much slower process. (USMC)

Ground crewmen manhandle a 250 pound Snakeye bomb at Chu Lai, while a third man prepares the bomb's nose fuses. Fuses had to be handled carefully both to prevent accidents and to ensure they worked properly. (USMC)

By 3 August 1966, VMFA-115 was delivering its three-millionth pound of ordnance against the communists. Master Sergeant Raymond W. Smith watched PFC George L. Brown install the fuse on the bomb that set the record. (USMC)

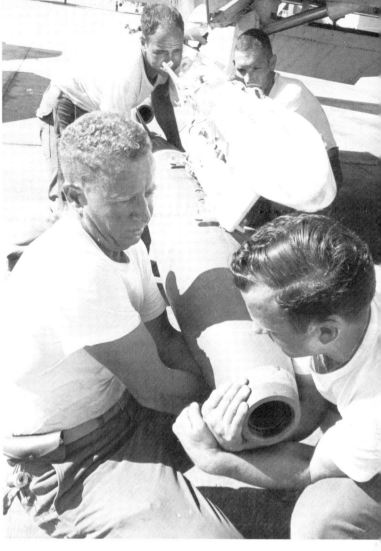

During Operation STARLITE in August of 1965, air support missions were flown almost non-stop. To quickly turn around the Phantoms, ground crews hand loaded the bombs; even 500 pounders! (USMC)

A pair of F-4Bs from VMFA-542 Bengals enroute to targets above the DMZ. They were accompanied by a Tactical Air Coordinator in a TA-4. The TACs flew higher performance jets than FACs, who flew O-1 Bird Dogs, allowing TACs to control strikes against targets in higher threat environments. (USMC)

Manny Simpson and his RIO man their F-4B Phantom at Danang for a mission against communist troops in I Corps. (Simpson)

MANNY SIMPSON

Manny (Manliff) Simpson joined the Marine Corps when he graduated from High School, taking advantage of the Platoon Leaders Course offered by the Marines. During 1959, the United States had the draft and it was a pretty good bet that you were going to do your duty for your country for at least two years in the service of its choice...unless you exercised the options offered by joining up before your number came up in the draft. The Marine Corps PLC was one of the best programs being offered at the time. Under this program, you attended boot camp during two of your college summer vacations. Then, upon graduation from college, you were commissioned a 2nd Lieutenant in the Marine Corps.

Manny's father had flown F6F Hellcats for the Navy during World War II and he convinced Manny that becoming a Naval Aviator was his best choice. So when he graduated from the University of Illinois in September of 1964, Manny was sent to Pensacola to begin flight training. The process of creating Naval Aviators from eager young men, many of whom (like Manny) had never even been in an airplane, is an intense procedure. Ground school at Pensacola, primary in the T-34 at Saufley Field, on to jets (if your grades are high enough...otherwise helicopters or transports) at Meridian, Mississippi, flying the T-2 Buckeye. Basic formation, instruments and finally carrier qualifications on the USS LEXINGTON in the Gulf of Mexico. Then on to Kingsville, Texas, where the art of flying fighters is refined in the F9F-8T Cougar. If you survive, you will get your wings two years after entering the program.

One of the best things about the Marine Corps program at that time was the choice of assignments offered you when you received your wings. As Manny said, "There just weren't that many of us and you pretty much had your choice of where you wanted to go." The basic choices were MCAS El Toro, California; MCAS Cherry Point, North Carolina; or MCAS Beaufort, South Carolina. Most graduates were opting for sunny California, but Manny consulted the instructors, who advised him that if he wanted to get a lot of flying, he should go to Beaufort. Since the Vietnam War was beginning to heat up and he felt sure he would be sent to Southeast Asia, Manny decided his best bet would be to go to Beaufort and gain as much experience as possible before going to war. When he reported in at Beaufort, he was given his choice of squadrons. He could pick the single-seat A-4 or F-8, or he could fly the Navy/Marine Corps newest and hottest fighter...the F-4B Phantom II. He chose the Phantom and was assigned to VMFA-251. His choice of Beaufort paid off in extra flying...150 hours more than the average "new guy" by the time he arrived in South Vietnam.

But before he left for Southeast Asia, he was chosen to fill one of the many quotas each squadron is allocated for training purposes. The quota slot was for one attendee at the Marine Corps Forward Air Control school. Graduates were qualified to serve with ground units, since the Marine Corps figured that pilots would make the most effective use of air support because they were familiar with its capabilities and limitations. The school lasted two months and a week after graduation, Manny was on his way to Vietnam. His narrative of some of the highlights of his tour follows:

When I reported to MAG-32 (Marine Air Group 32) at Chu Lai during 1967, there were three F-4 squadrons on the station. I was assigned to VMFA-542 and the first words out of the C.O.'s mouth were, "Boy, am I glad to see you!" The squadron had eighteen airplanes and twelve pilots. They had not had any replacements for months and the normal rotational attrition had whittled their strength down to about half of what it should have been.

I had been there a couple of days and was well into my 'in-country' training, when the C.O. called me into his office. He said, "You're not going to believe this, but we got hit with one of these quota things again and I have to send someone to a ground unit as a FAC. I don't want to send one of my experienced pilots, since I am already unable to meet my mission requirements so...you're it!" He was pretty smart though, because the Marines also had rule that said you couldn't serve as a FAC unless you had been in-country for at least six months. He figured that he would send me up there, thereby fulfilling his quota, and when they discovered that I was a new guy, they would send me back and call up the next unit on the list. His parting words were, "Make damn sure you tell them you haven't been here very long!"

Well, sure enough, I got sent down to the 1st Battalion, 1st Marines, outside of Danang. After about a week, I mentioned that I had only been in-country for a couple of weeks. They said, "Well, this is all screwed up, and we're going to have to check on it." But in the meantime, I got to go out on several missions with the ground pounders and saw how they operated. It was very interesting...not what I was trained for and not something that I wanted to do on a regular basis...but interesting. It took the upper echelon about a month to decide that they had made a mistake and another two weeks to get the paper work processed, but just like the C.O. had predicted, I was back in the squadron within two months. This time, I stayed there.

When I returned to the squadron, I discovered that they were not much better off, manpower-wise, than when I left. From May until November of 1967 I was with VMFA-542. When they rotated to Japan, I stayed in country and was transferred to the General Staff at Danang. While there, I flew missions with VMFA-122.

VMFA-542 flew a lot of missions into North Vietnam, but rarely went to Pack Six. We did go to Vinh though and that was a real bad area, as was the northern part of Laos, up around Tchepone. We took a lot of hits in those areas. When I flew with VMFA-122, we flew a lot of BARCAP missions...air-to-air stuff... up in the Pack Six area. 542's missions were almost always pure air-to-ground — interdiction or close air support. We had to maintain hot pads, with the crews manning the airplanes, twenty-four hours a day to be able to react to close air support for troops in contact with the enemy. With the hot pad manned, we could get airborne within a minute. In our primary area of operations, we could reach those kinds of targets within a few minutes.

Most of the ground fire we saw was automatic weapons, small arms. Everything from AK-47s to 50 calibers...quad fifties, and some 20MM. There were a few spots in the mountains where they would shoot at you with some heavier stuff. These were areas that contained permanent NVA base camps...places like the Ashau Valley and Khe Sanh...that was where you would see flak. I don't remember exactly how many airplanes we lost during that period, but between the three squadrons, it was quite a few. Because of the circumstances, we were never sure exactly what happened to a lot of them. Most of our losses in 542 were due to ground fire and I would guess that we lost nine or ten airplanes during my tour. Out of that total, about half of the crews got out and were picked up. I personally saw three of them go down and all were hit by nothing larger than 50 caliber. The thing about that was, you didn't always know they were shooting at you. Sometimes they would fire tracers and you would see them going by the canopy...maybe you would hear a couple of hits, but in most cases, you just didn't realize you were being shot at unless the ground FAC told you they were shooting at you. Many, many times I returned from a mission with holes in the airplane without even realizing I was taking fire.

I can remember a couple of cases of guys ejecting, then providing close air support to keep the enemy away until the helos could come in and drag them out. But I remember many more where they just went straight in. In those cases, you never knew what happened. We supposed it was ground fire that got them, but we never knew for sure. After all, you are flying so fast, so close to the ground, and when something happens...you get hit...or you are concentrating on a target...or get distracted by any number of things...and the next thing you know, you bore a smoking hole in the ground.

We flew a lot of night missions. We flew 'TPQ' missions up north and, for about two months in the middle of my tour, I flew two missions a night...every night. These missions were laid on to react to fresh intelligence. For instance, a recce flight that day would spot a new SAM site or truck park in central or southern North Vietnam and we would be fragged to hit it. I would normally go down for briefing about 2330, take off for the first mission about 0100, fly for an hour and a half, come back, brief and take off again. You usually got back from the second hop about 0600, just in time for breakfast. I did that every day...seven days a week...for two months...with no time off for good behavior ...good weather, bad weather...it didn't matter, we went.

One of toughest missions I flew occurred during the late Fall of 1967. We normally maintained a hot pad twenty-four hours a day, so that we could react to calls for help from troops in contact with the enemy. But during this period, they shut down the runway at Chu Lai for repairs. In order to maintain our sortie rate and provide the close air support the ground pounders needed, we operated off of the taxiway. At that time of the war, there was a lot of pressure from Washington to produce numbers...sorties, tonnage of bombs, body counts, enemy vehicles or structures destroyed...that sort of thing. In order to produce those numbers, we were operating fully loaded F-4s off of a taxiway, which was not very wide, was certainly not level and had no arresting gear at the end of it. So, if you had a problem, you were dead...there was just no way to stop. Fortunately, our guys were good and we were doing this only during the daytime, so we didn't lose anybody. With the runway repairs going on, we didn't have any lights on the airport at all. For all intents and purposes, the base was shut down at night. So, even though we were manning the

hot pad at night, the situation was very loose. People were not in that "ready for action mode" they normally acquired on the hot pad.

On the night of my toughest mission, it was particularly loose. The weather was very bad. Danang was zero-zero, and shut down. Practically no one was flying anywhere in the I Corps area of South Vietnam. At Chu Lai, the ceiling was less than 100 feet and heavy rain showers, driven by gale-force winds, had reduced visibility to less than a mile. This was not flying weather! I was sitting in the club, when I got a call from the hot pad. They were trying to get up a bridge game and one of the pilots did not play bridge. They asked me if I would come down and fill in for him. I did and he went on up to the club and started drinking. (Fortunately, I had not had my first drink when I got the call from the bridge players.) We had not been playing very long when the phone rang.

Now, ordinarily when the phone rings in the alert shack, it means trouble. We all wore our flight gear...harness, G-suit, survival vest and weapons while on alert. Then, when the phone rang, the pilots would run to the airplanes while the RIOs got the mission information. The RIO would man the airplane while the pilot started the engines and be strapping in while the pilot taxied out. This made for real quick reaction, which was often the difference between life and death for troops in contact. If things were particularly busy, the airplanes might even be manned on the hot pad. Things were so loose on this night that we didn't even have our flight gear on when the phone rang.

One of the backseaters picked up the phone and listened for a minute, then hung up. Someone had called for close air support, but with the weather the way it was and with no runway to fly off of, he thought it was someone calling from the club as a joke and hung up. Well, the phone rang right away again and when he picked it up, the same guy was on the line and he sounded like this was anything but a joke. He covered the mouthpiece, looked at me and said, "I think this guy is serious about our flying." I took the phone from him and asked the guy on the other end how in hell he expected us to fly under the circumstances. He didn't know anything about our circumstances. All he knew was that a company of good guys had walked into the middle of a battalion of NVA regulars in the hills northwest of Chu Lai and if they didn't get some support soon, they weren't going to be there in the morning.

Danang was zero-zero...there was no flying there at all and we were about their last hope. That really puts the pressure on you to do something. We talked it over and decided it would be nearly impossible...but every time you decided you couldn't do it, you kept thinking about those guys out there getting chewed up by the NVA. We finally decided to give it a try. We got a bunch of jeeps lined up on the taxiway and used their lights to get us airborne. I had twelve 500 pound napalm bombs on my airplane and my wingman had twelve 500 pound Snakeyes. As we blasted off and turned out over the club at fifty feet, I can still remember the glimpse I got of the guys standing out in that

With empty MERs on the inboard wing stations, MAJ John Hubner rolls out with his drag chute deployed, on return to Chu Lai after a mission against VC troops who had attacked Republic of Korea Marines in I Corps on 11 June 1967. (USMC)

A newly arrived F-4B Phantom of VMFA-542 on the ramp at Danang. When the US buildup in Vietnam began during 1965, Danang was the only airfield in northern South Vietnam capable of handling jet fighter traffic. It had a 10,000 foot runway and a parallel taxiway.

During one twenty-two day period in the Spring of 1966 VMFA-542 dropped over a million pounds of ordnance on communist positions. Each man in the ordnance shop handled more than 2,000 pounds of bombs per day during this period. The commander of VFMA-542, LTCOL Eddie E. Pearcy, dropped the bomb that set the one-millionth pound record on 29 March 1966. (USMC)

Loaded with Mk 82 Snakeye bombs, CAPT John McCord heads for the target on a 31 July 1967 mission against a concentration of VC. The VC had been spotted in a box canyon by a FAC and the mission resulted in fourteen confirmed kills for VMFA-542. (USMC)

rainstorm waving at us...like they were waving good-bye...they really thought we were nuts.

We knew that we had to stay under the overcast, because if we got up into the soup, we would never be able to punch back down in the target area. So we flew out over the water and went up the coast at fifty to 100 feet. I could hardly believe it when the the controllers put me in touch with some idiot that was flying around up there in a helicopter. I don't know where he came from, but he was trying to coordinate the air support for the mission. He kept telling me how bad the weather was in that area and that there were mountains all around his position. I said, "I don't know how we are going to do you any good if you are in the mountains...I don't know if I can even get to you staying under the clouds, but I'll give it a try." He told me that the ceiling was a little higher in that area and that if we could just sneak under the stuff until we got to where he was, maybe we could do him some good.

Well, that's what we did. There were times when I am sure I was no more than fifty feet off the deck, doing 400 knots...at night...in the rain, with no horizon. All you could see were shadows and stuff. Just as I was about to give up on it, I spotted the flashes from the fire-fight and got a much better perspective on where we were. When we got into their area, the ceiling picked up 500 to 1,000 feet. Visibility was still bad, but we did have some room to operate. It was weird...all around us, the clouds were practically on the ground, but right here in this area, it was almost like a big, domed, stadium.

The troops were dug into the base of a mountain and were really catching it from three sides. The mountain they were on was one of many in the area and we were forced to fly around them and through valleys to maintain any kind of a pattern. As soon as we got into the area, we turned off our navigation lights, because they REALLY started shooting at us. At one point, I called my wingman and told him that he was drawing a lot of fire. He said, "Oh yeah? Well, you oughta see what it looks like over where you are!" They could hear us, but they couldn't see us. That didn't stop them from shooting and they obviously did not have a shortage of ammo.

The bombing pattern we set up went something like this; we would come down, pickle, break left, then right, fly around the hill they were on...which took about three minutes, break out on the other side, turn left, extend for about twenty seconds, turn around, try to pick up the target, run in, drop, turn left and right again to fly around the mountain. It was sort of an open figure eight. As soon as you dropped, you had to break to avoid running into the mountain. You had to break left, start to go through the hills, then break right, go around the hill in a right hand circle, come out the other way, break left again, go out a little ways to pick up your new target line, then turn and start in all over. All of this at altitudes which varied from 50 to 900 feet and at 400 to 500 knots of airspeed.

The problem we had when we first got into the area was that we couldn't tell the good guys from the bad guys. Everyone was shooting and there were tracers and shells going off everywhere. They all looked the same to us at our altitude and speed. Another concern was running into that helicopter. The guy stayed in the area and we never did see him! He kept saying, "I know where you are, I know where you are!" I said, "I hope to hell you do, because at this speed, I'll never see you!" He did manage to stay clear and most of the conversation was now with the guy on the ground, who kept trying to direct us in. I didn't want to just drop without having a pretty good idea of where they were, but he said, "Look, if you don't drop something, we are never going to get out of here anyway, so just drop something and we'll see where it goes and direct you from there!" I didn't want to do that. I was afraid I was going to hit some of the good guys. He said, "Well, it won't make any difference." The resignation in his voice finally convinced me that I had to drop something.

We had completed one pass and were turning in for another without having dropped anything, when there was a big flash. I asked him what the hell that was. He said, "Didja see that? That was THEM!" That gave me an aiming point and I didn't take my eyes off it until I had pickled off my first napes. Luckily, I scored a hit on their ammo dump and the whole world turned to daylight as I pulled off the target...it was just like high noon! Well, now we had a marker to work off of and they started directing us according to that big fire. We were able to do some good bombing, but the problem was, they could see us and we were really taking some murderous fire. In fact, my airplane was so shot up that it was a write-off when we finally got it back.

Unfortunately, on one of those passes, my wingman went in. I don't have any idea of what happened. One second he was there, the next he was not. Under those conditions, it could have been ground fire, or he just flew into a mountain. Like I said, I was losing fuel and my electrical and hydraulic systems were in bad shape. In the F-4 you have three control systems: PC-1, PC-2, and the utility system. My PC-1 was shot out, and PC-2 showed a fluctuating needle. I told the guy on the ground that I had to get the hell out of there. Since I was losing fuel, I knew that I was going to have to climb to make it back to Danang. I couldn't go to Chu Lai...there was just no way to land on that taxiway at night, with no lights, no arresting gear and the possibility of having no brakes. Halfway to Danang, I lost my cockpit lights! There I was, in solid instrument conditions and couldn't see the instruments!

We used to carry a little pen light flashlight around our necks on a string during night missions and that saved me. I was able to get it turned on and I ripped off my mask to hold the light between my teeth. Hell, we were really having problems! I couldn't talk on the radio with that flashlight in my mouth, so my RIO called up Danang and asked for a GCA approach. Well, they didn't even know anybody was flying and they were pretty much shut down. They had some young, inexperienced kid in the GCA van, who was not expecting any business that night. He said, "Who is this?" When we told him, he said, "You mean you're FLYING?" I'll never forget that...the surprise in his voice..then he said he didn't know how to do this...he would have to find someone who did...and he left! I thought, "Oh great! Here I am in the soup, with a flashlight in my mouth and this guy is going off the air!"

Just when I was figuring we were going to have to jump out over the water, in a driving rainstorm, in the middle of the night, a clear confident voice came over the radio, telling us that they had us on radar and giving us our first turn to the GCA course. This guy was one of the best controllers I had ever heard. I told him we were losing fuel and would probably only have one shot at the landing. He told us that they had no ceiling and so he would not be able to tell us that we were going to break out and see the runway. I said it didn't matter...we were landing and he better have us on the runway centerline, or he was going to have a crash on his hands. Well, he did. He brought us right down the glide path...right on the centerline and I touched down without ever seeing the runway. I kept it straight using the compass and got on the brakes gingerly. I had never done anything like this in an airplane before. Of course, when you fly the simulator, you take off and land using your heading indicator, but there really isn't any runway to run off of and you are not going to roll yourself up in a flaming ball of aluminum if you blow your heading a little bit.

When we touched down, I lost everything...all electrical...everything. The world just got real quiet, except for the thump and bump of the landing gear as I sweated the roll-out. When the airplane stopped, I opened the canopy and it was dead-quiet. The fog was so bad, you couldn't see more than a few feet in front of you. I had no idea of where I was...I didn't even know which runway he had landed us on. When we got down from the airplane, you could walk four feet from the airplane

The MOREST arresting gear crew at Chu Lai talks to a Phantom on final approach for an arrested landing during December of 1967. The MOREST gear saved a number of Phantoms that would have otherwise crashed due to battle damage. (USMC)

and not see it! I could hear sirens off in the distance and wondered what was going on. As it turned out, they were looking for us. They had gotten confused and were looking on the wrong end of the runway. Without a radio, we couldn't tell them where we were...even if we had known. We started walking and finally walked into the side of a hangar. That was the thickest fog I had ever seen!

All of this is not the most interesting part of the whole story. I eventually flew over 300 combat missions and came home. I got out of the Marine Corps, went to law school, got my law degree and started my own practice. One day during 1978, I was sitting in my office when I got a call from one of my partners, informing me that General Motors was interviewing area law firms to determine who would represent General Motors Acceptance Corporation in the six-county Chicago area. One of my partners knew someone and this was a courtesy interview. We were hopeful, but doubtful about chances to get their account, since we were a small firm at the time. On the day of the interview, I got tied up and was late getting to the office. The General Motors lawyers were already there when I arrived and the head of their contingent was taking a special interest in all the Marine Corps momentos and airplane pictures I had hanging on the office wall.

His name was Ramirez and he was a Vietnam Veteran who had also come home, gone to law school and moved up in his profession. His first question to me, when I finally showed up, was, "What was your call sign?" I am sure that's the last thing anyone would expect to hear. I was afraid everyone would be pretty upset that I was late for what was the most important meeting we had had to that date. I said, "Castor Oil, why?" "I thought so...you flew F-4s, didn't you?" "Yeah, why?" "Where were you on the night of September 9th and 10th, 1967?"

A U.S. Air Force F-4C Phantom of the 366th TFW makes the 1,000th arrested landing using the Marines' MOREST arresting gear at Danang Air Base on 5 January 1967. (USMC)

CAPT Manny Simpson's Phantom of VMFA-542 is hauled to a stop by the MOREST system at Chu Lai, on 9 September 1967. Construction at Chu Lai was begun on 9 May 1965 and eventually, an 8,000 foot SATS (Short Airfield Tactical Support) runway and a catapult was installed. The runway was operational on 9 April 1966. (USMC photo by SSgt Gary Thomas)

CAPT Manny Simpson is congratulated after being presented with the thirteenth star to his Air Medal awarded for combat missions flown in both North and South Vietnam. (Simpson)

Well, that's not the kind of mission you forget about and I was able tell him where I was. He said, "You're the guy who saved my life that night...let's go have some coffee." Everyone around that table looked stunned, but we just walked out of the meeting and had coffee. All he talked about was that night and I had a chance for the first time to experience what it was like for him on the ground. I wouldn't have traded places with him for anything! Funny thing, he said he wouldn't have traded places with us either, considering the weather. He said he thought we were crazy! He had tried for years to track me down, but never got anywhere with the Marine Corps. He told me he thought we had a good chance to get their account. I said, "Well, aren't you interested in what our qualifications are?" He said, 'If you can do what you did on that night...you can sure do this!" We have had the account ever since and our relationship with General Motors has grown substantially, providing us with numerous other large commercial accounts.

That was a beneficial result of the war and some of the darkly humorous things that happened during my tour also make it easier to remember. One that stands out in my mind happened at Danang. My roommate was scheduled to fly one of the squadron "hangar queens" that day. (Author's note: A hangar queen is an airplane which is plagued with seemingly insoluble gremlins. Pilot after pilot will write the airplane up and the maintenance crews will spend countless hours trying to duplicate these glitches so they can be fixed. Somehow, they never do.) I was sitting in our hootch reading, when he returned about an hour after takeoff. That might not have been unusual if the mission had just been scrubbed, but he was soaking wet. I asked him what had happened. Well, he was in a blue funk and just muttered, "Nothing". I kept pressing him and he finally said, "Well, I punched out of the damn thing!" Shortly after takeoff, while on initial climb out over the bay, all those gremlins finally concentrated their efforts and a wing had just blown off! He had landed in shallow water, waded ashore, dumped his parachute and survival vest and walked back to the squadron. We could hear the sirens as the base emergency vehicles rushed around looking for him.

After a shower and change to a dry flight suit, he took off towards the flight line. He wasn't talking to anybody, but by then everyone knew he had gone in and, as he walked along, he picked up a crowd who wanted to know what had happened. Without a word to any of them, he walked straight to the squadron maintenance shack, asked for the clipboard containing the maintenance records of his former mount, drew a big down arrow on the face of the sheet, and said, "Duplicate that, you S.O.B.!" And without another word, he went to the officer's club and got drunk.

I had been over there about a year and like so many of the guys, had become cynical about the war. That, of course, leads to a level of insubordination that is intolerable to those who have not had to lay their lives on the line on a daily basis. They wanted to reassign me to FAC duty with the line troops again and I was resisting. Fortunately, I knew General Anderson and one of the colonels on the wing staff was a real good friend. He called and told me that he had a position open on the staff and wondered if I was interested. Well, it beat hell out of being a FAC, so I took the job. My experiences on the wing staff showed me another side of the war.

The staff side was completely different from the operational end. When you were flying missions, you were exposing yourself to danger, but you could really feel you were doing a job that could make a difference in the war effort. The staff experience was the stuff of a Catch 22-type novel. After serving on the wing staff, it was easy for me to see why the rear echelon was the target of bitter resentment by those who actually did the fighting.

I reported to the General and he asked me to extend my tour. I agreed and he assigned me as a sort of unofficial aide. My job was to keep track of where we dropped bombs and what kind of activity was occurring in I Corps. We got along pretty well and I would provide him with off-the-record briefings early in the morning on what was really happening. Then we would go into the official staff briefing and I would lie to him because the colonels would tell me what to say.

One of the first things I discovered was that there was no large scale map of North and South Vietnam which would show all of this information in a graphic manner. During briefings, when you read off the coordinates of some activity, everyone would pull out their maps and try to locate the spot; then when the activity shifted to another map, they would have to go through the same exercise again, meanwhile trying to keep the big picture in their heads. I thought this was insane, so I took it upon my self to put together a big map, one which virtually covered my whole office wall, of Vietnam. Well, this kind of organization attracted a lot of attention and before you knew it my desk had become the focal point of wing headquarters. Everyone was in there looking at that map, putting their greasy fingerprints on it, which encouraged me to go out and get some acetate protection.

The colonels were so enamoured of my organizational ability that they decided I should keep track of all the bombs dropped in the war, using the 8 digit map coordinates. I considered the thousands of bombs being dropped and decided that, even with 20 or 30 staff people working for me, it would be an impossible task and one which would be meaningless to our effort, because we would only end up with reams of paper, which no one would take the time to collate in a meaningful manner. I balked. The colonels went to the general, and asked for an explanation. I told him how ridiculous it was, and while I was at it, told him what a bunch of idiots some of these colonels were. Well, the general was a diplomat as well as a military man. He treated me like a headstrong son instead of an insubordinate junior officer, explaining that sometimes you just had to accept a certain level of incompetence and that it was better to go along with it...as long as it didn't get anyone killed. The result of that meeting was that I devised a system of color-coded symbols that we put on the map daily to indicate what kinds of ordnance was dropped and where it was dropped.

Well, when you really stopped to think about what all this was accomplishing, it was a joke. It was just one more attempt to keep score in a game we really weren't trying to win. They thought that if we put enough colored dots on the map, that would show that we were winning. Unfortunately, that mentality sometimes carried over to the bombing. If we dropped enough bombs, we would accomplish something. It didn't really matter where we put the dots (or the bombs), as long as we put enough of them on the map.

Armament specialists install safety pins into AIM-7 Sparrow and AIM-9 Sidewinder air-to-air missiles on an VMFA-122 Phantom which has just returned from a combat mission on 8 February 1968. (USMC)

The object of this was to make the local planners feel good about their efforts. The overall effort was managed from 10,000 miles away and field commanders really didn't have the authority to fight the war as if we meant to win, so it didn't much matter where we put the dots...and we knew it. The adornment of the map continued for weeks, until it was really overloaded with dots, literally thousands and thousands of them.

Then one day a Saigon headquarters type stopped by on one of their rare field inspections. He was so impressed with my map that he decided that he had to take it back to Saigon for an official briefing for higher headquarters. When I went to the General to protest that their briefing would be based on false or misleading information, he replied, "Well, what difference will it make?" He was right, of course.

This captured Czech M-53 twin 30MM anti-aircraft gun was displayed during the ARVN Armed Forces Day at the Sports Arena in Danang on 25 June 1969. This gun was typical of the type of weapons encountered by Marine Phantoms on Close Air Support (CAS) missions. (USMC)

An RF-4B of VMCJ-1 on final approach to Danang. VMCJ-1 began receiving the photo reconnaissance version of the Phantom in October of 1966. The Marines were the only service to use the RF-4B.

Ground crews signal the pilot of a VMCJ-1 RF-4B Phantom to shut down the engines after returning to Danang from a mission over South Vietnam. The replacement of the RF-8 by the RF-4B enabled the Marines to conduct night reconnaissance missions. (USMC)

A VMCJ-1 Phantom rolls out at Danang after a March of 1967 mission. The squadron set a record for flight hours in a single month, flying 1,102 hours during March alone. (USMC)

Photo Phantoms are parked in hardened shelters at Danang during January of 1970. VMCJ-1 was one of the first fixed wing Marine squadrons to deploy to Vietnam and remained in-country for five years. (USMC photo by SGT A.J. May)

VMCJ-1 RF-4Bs flew reconnaissance missions over both North and South Vietnam. By 1970, the increased surface-to-air missile threat required them to carry ECM pods on the inboard wing stations. (USMC photo by SGT R.W. Nelson)

(Above) Crash crews spray fire fighting foam onto an RF-4B of VMCJ-1 at Danang after the starboard main landing gear failed to extend. Without a starboard wheel, the Phantom landed on the starboard wing tank, spilling fuel out onto the runway. (USMC by MAJ R. Hamilton)

(Below) The Phantom was towed back to the VMCJ-1 flight line and placed on jacks for repairs to its landing gear and starboard fuselage. Although severely damaged, the Phantom was repaired and later returned to service. (USMC by LCPL R. Nelson)

The forward firing oblique camera station in the RF-4B mounted a KS-86-A camera which recorded everything along the F-4s flight path, providing a photographic record of the mission route. (USMC)

VMCJ-1 maintenance personnel position a J-79 engine on its dolly for installation into one of the squadron's RF-4Bs at Danang during January of 1970. J-79 engines powered all US variants of the Phantom. (USMC)

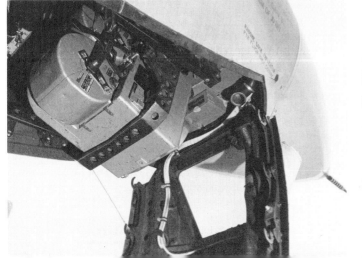

21

JOHN VERDI

The next three narratives in this chronicle of Marine Corps Phantoms in Vietnam are by former members of VMFA-122, which was commanded by COL John Verdi. COL Verdi declined to be interviewed for this book. Instead, he suggested that I research some papers he had contributed to the Marine Corps Historical Center. Under most other circumstances, one interview, more or less, would not make much difference to the story, but Verdi's impact on the squadron was so profound that the story of VMFA-122 during its combat tour (1967-68) needs to be illuminated by his personal recollections. From his writings I have drawn what I consider to be pertinent segments, in order to draw a picture of this brilliant tactician and maverick military genius.

Verdi incited intense feelings among his troops, both pro and con; however, they all agreed that John Verdi was a single-minded soldier, completely dedicated to the task at hand. That was a very tough thing to be during the Vietnam War, where vacillation was raised to a fine art by the politicians who ran the war.

In order to give the reader a better understanding of Verdi's personal philosophy, I have excerpted portions of a book review he wrote during 1984. John Verdi was retired from the Marine Corps when he was asked by MAJ Eugene Oster, USMC (Ret) to review a book for the Marine Corps Historical Foundation. The book was "WAR IN THE SHADOWS - The Guerilla in History," by Robert B. Asprey, which had been published by Doubleday & Co. in two volumes during 1975. His review was sent in memo form and left no doubt about Verdi's personal philosophy:

The word "liberal" has been intentionally omitted from the text of enclosure (1). I have instead borrowed one of the more colorful maledictions of revolutionary socialism: ROTTENINTELLECTUAL; wherewith to label subject author and sympathizers whomsoever. Had my late friend, (Oster) who really was liberal, lived long enough the first thought which I would have communicated to him is drawn from his own Prussian provenance. In the Prussian military tradition, it is a part of an officer's duty to criticize his general's orders (bluntly and without fear of reprisal); but it is no part of his duty (or his general's) to criticize the settled policy of their sovereign. A liberal tradition thereby sets limits on dissent. The rottenintellectual acknowledges neither these nor any limits. Accordingly, in well-regulated societies (of which a contemporary example is the Soviet society), authors of "histories" hostile to the policies of the State stand, as a minimum, to be stripped of honors and titles; and may expect further to be stripped of citizenship, identity, and life itself.

Squadron portrait of VMFA-122 at Danang during 1967. LTCOL John Verdi, squadron commander, is in the front cockpit, while his RIO, Julie Steinon, is in the rear cockpit. Jack McEncroe is kneeling at far right. (Jack McEncroe)

To those of the distribution who may be disposed to take offence from some (or all) of this letter of transmittal and enclosures I make two affirmations:
a. I do not imagine that all intellectuals are rottenintellectuals; nor have I suggested that they are. The same may be said for institutions. BUT...
b. Subject "history" is offensive to me as soldier and as citizen, in detail and in sum; and I have judged its author and his individual and institutional collaborators accordingly.

FROM VERDI'S COMMENTARY IN DETAIL:

On selected heros....and villains. One of the differences between history (what happened) and propaganda (what we would like people to think happened) is that the former tells us who won and who lost (and if complete may even tell us why); while the latter presumes to tell us who should have won and who should have lost (and thereby becomes to some degree, or entirely, fictional). Thus history disdains heros and villains alike; and propaganda is immediately identifiable by the partisan labels stuck to its drantis personae (as this two-volume "history"). Per exemplum:

Hero Ho: Ere you be moved to drip a tear over the "Prison Poem," read over the record (most carefully documented by Bernard Fall; most mordantly attested by Dramesi) of the treatment of POW's by Hero Ho and his hierarchy; and then ask yourself: "Would Hero Ho have survived a sojourn in one of his own camps?"

Hero Giap: In 1969, the only thing Giap could have been "preparing" (p. 1305) was strategy for his own reassertion, having for the three years following the battle of Khe Sanh been relegated to the status of non-person.

(Author's note: In another paper, Verdi made the following comments on Khe Sanh, which was widely compared to Dien Bien Phu by the liberal media in the United States while the battle raged. Verdi flew C-119s in support of the French in 1954.)

AMPLIFYING COMMENT on Khe Sanh compared to Dien Bien Phu: Ten years ago I was asked to give a talk to the British United Services Club in Los Angeles. For subject I selected Khe Sanh and for emphasis compared the successful defense thereof to the failure of the French Union Forces at Dien Bien Phu. For references I used SHORE's excellent monograph on Khe Sanh and FALL's "L'Enfer Dans Un Tout Petit Endroit" (Hell in a Very Small Place) on Dien Bien Phu, both of which I was able to augment with personal observations, having been a participant in both campaigns.

The important differences between the two situations are these:

1. There were 14,000 troops in Dien Bien Phu; only 5,000 (max) in Khe Sanh.

2. Dien Bien Phu was 160 miles west of Hanoi (and we actually resupplied Castor from Haiphong, 44 miles farther east); Khe Sanh was 23 miles from Dong Ha and 58 miles from Phu Bai. The Viet Minh resupplied from sanctuary (China) only 75 miles distant; the NVA troops at Khe Sanh were precariously situated at the end of a 500 mile long supply line; accordingly, at Khe Sanh, it was the enemy's supply problem which proved intractable, not ours.

3. Forces available for relief of Dien Bien Phu (i.e, mobile reserve) amounted to only 4,000 troops, and, in the event, these got no closer than Luang Prabang (100 miles away); relief forces available for lifting the seige of Khe Sanh amounted to many times the number inside the Khe Sanh perimeter and, in the event, were not required.

4. Tactical aircraft available to support French Union forces numbered one for every 1,000 troops; to support American troops, we had TEN TIMES the number of aircraft.

5. Clausewitz sensibly advises against situating a fortress on the enemy's side of a mountain range...nevertheless, that is what the French did at Dien Bien Phu. What more need be said?

After his failure at Khe Sanh, Giap became a non-person for THREE YEARS. Given the orderly mind-set of revolutionary socialism, this means he was responsible for the destruction of three divisions, or some 30,000 casualties, a loss the DRV could ill afford.

Verdi's criticism of the book continued;

On page 1307, Robert Asprey boasts, "The nation's press (were) too big and powerful" to be brought under control. Well, in other times and in other places, they have proven not so "too big and powerful": they were not "too big" for the NSDAP, nor "too powerful" for the CPSU. Charles Lindbergh had it right 50 years ago, when he said, "The greatest danger to the American Republic is THE PRESS". Our press certainly proved Lindbergh right in the years 1965-75.

After a long dissertation on the application of labels, Verdi cites the following personal experience:

As for "depravity", consider the following memoir: On 4 June 1954, the "chargement" (load) to be hauled from Cat Bi (Haiphong) to Ton Son Nhut (Saigon) was 72 prisoners (Vietminh). As "chef-de-bord" (plane commander) for this leg, it was my responsibility to specify aircraft configuration, fuel on board, disposition of cargo, and crew coordination. The officer responsible for processing my requests was the OC, CRA (Compagnie Ravitaillement par Air): named Patch. What I told Patch was that I wanted the doors removed (the aft clamshells, not the later air-delivery door) and the prisoners rigged as air-drop cargo (i.e.trussed up and tied down by twelves on six pallets) so that we could jettison them in the event of a problem. Now Patch was a very tough guy: tougher than any of his troops, which was how he maintained discipline; but my request was too heavy for him, especially after I explained that I was not worried about their overpowering us and making off with the airplane (Patch had detailed us four guards armed with automatic weapons). What I was worried about was a 600 mile trip over terrain elevations up to 10,000 feet in a C-119 with seventy-eight people on board and that amount of fuel necessary to take us to destination and alternate, at which combination of gross weight and density altitude this airplane would not be capable of maintaining cruising altitude on one engine (should we have to shut the other one down for any reason); and as these were C-119C airplanes in 1954, they did not have the crew escape chute forward; and even if the crew did succeed in getting past the prisoners and out the personnel doors aft, it was a fair bet all of us would not walk out of the jungle. Inasmuch as the prisoners would die with the airplane anyway under these circumstances, it seemed more reason-

McEncroe's Phantom carries a typical combat load of six Mk 82 500 pound Snakeye bombs, a Vulcan 20MM cannon pod on the centerline station and Sidewinder and Sparrow AAMs for self-defense. (McEncroe)

able to me to rig them as jettisonable cargo, so that if we lost an engine we could dump them and save the airplane as well as the crew.

Brutal? Yes...but so was the contingency. But "depraved"? These were not Giap's regulars captured in the field of battle; they were irregulars, and they were already the beneficiaries not of mere courtesy but of MERCY...mercy shown them by the "depraved" French army, mercy which, in the person of Patch, proved unyielding to my representation of the cold, hard facts of C-119 performance. So they rode to Saigon as passengers and not (as I would have had them) as cargo; and happily, we had no enroute emergencies. But in the same circumstances, I would make the same request again...and would, of course, thereby stand to be abused by the likes of Robert Asprey as "depraved".

Commenting on American policy in Vietnam, Verdi wrote:

Well, the late Robinson Jeffers said it best. He described the United States of America thus:
'Eagle beak and talons,...... Brain of chicken.....'
Whence we should not have expected "Eagle beak and talons" (Rolling Thunder) to accomplish useful results under the direction of 'Brain of Chicken' (Robert Strange McNamara ... and his boss).

Verdi's most caustic indictment of the book is contained in the paragraph headed:

On History: A consistent, conscientious, and comprehensive confutation of all the fallacies and falsehoods put forth in the 1,475 pages of these two volumes would call for a veritable St Dominic of military history, a small army of clerks and scribes, and a lifetime of dedication...none of which (nor any combination) this reviewer is able to bring to the task. Accordingly from Asprey's necronomicon only those examples are treated infra which have appeared most flagrant and which can be quickly dealt with.

Verdi's idea of "quickly dealt with" ran to thirteen single-space typed pages. His scholarship and intellect are evident throughout. His credentials as military philosopher are established with such items as his comparison of the soldier with the policeman. (Since the United States has become the policeman of the world, we are required to act as policemen, not as soldiers when faced with war.)

THE SOLDIER may shoot first; THE POLICEMAN may not. Indeed, the soldier is conditioned and commanded to shoot first; but let not the policeman be tempted to try it....what it will get him is first an internal affairs investigation and next, criminal prosecution and civil complaint.

THE POLICEMAN, like THE SOLDIER, is sworn; but THE POLICEMAN is not enlisted and he is not commissioned, and so he may quit. Not so THE SOLDIER; and let him not even contemplate it, for the statute of limitations never runs out in the case of a deserter.

A VMFA-122 Phantom on final approach for landing at Atsugi, Japan, on 31 January 1971. When the US pullout from Vietnam began many Marine Phantom squadrons which had been stationed in Japan before 1965 returned to their former Japanese bases. (Shinichi Ohtaki)

THE SOLDIERS code is simple; there are only three RULES:

1. You must kill the enemy
2. You must not kill your comrades.
3. You must not kill yourself.

And all history discloses only one "WAR CRIME", and that is: to be a loser...

THE SOLDIER's reward is triumph, something THE POLICEMAN never achieves; for the policeman toils in a quicksand of codes endlessly multiplied and mutated. The Policeman never wins because it is not intended that he should win...in Soviet society, his token "enemy", the criminal, is the "social ally", whose defeat would put too many GPUshniks out of work! Our society is no better in this regard, as the criminal is kept in circulation to maintain the employment of a vast army of attorneys public and private...

These are the ruminations of a complex man. An intellectual. But also a dedicated soldier who served his country better than most. He was not universally loved, but all who served under him respected him for his skill as a pilot and his single-minded loyalty to his troops. Commenting on the conduct of the air war, he said:

GENERAL COMMENT on operational chronology:
At squadron level, we kept little more than a Unit Diary; and what I personally can recapture is taken from log-book entries, mission cards (all of which I kept), and memory (which, being selective and unreliable, I have tried to cross-check whenever possible).

I flew 265 missions during my tour 67-68, and memory confirms (by non-recall) the truism about "hours and hours of boredom punctuated by moments of pure panic." Some missions were very memorable (not all for good things, either); to these I have added a few words to mark some lesson. Most were not, even at the time...the middle-of-the-night sorties were often executed in a kind of trance, from which one fully awoke only when something went badly wrong. We arrived at DAG on 1 September 1967 and flew our first combat sorties on 4 September. First mission for each crew was with a 235 crew leading (including me, though I had flown combat during MAWTUPac TDY's in Aug of '65 and in Feb of '66). Later we performed the same orientation for 542 crews.

The Event numbers were assigned from the Wing Fragmentary Op Orders. Target coordinates are given to the nearest 100 meters from the 10,000 meter grid (i.e. six digits, not eight); for Pre-Planned missions, these are as briefed, but more often Pre-Planned missions were On-Call, or were changed to On-Call after contact was established with DASC or FAC, and for these the target coordinates were passed to the flight after mission completion (by FAC, ASRT, or DASC). Description of the target might (or might not) be included; and results depended on visual observation by FAC or FO (this was sometimes possible with TPQ, but most often was not). Occasionally, we would hear from a supported infantry unit (usually a day or more later) that we had made some specific contribution (e.g. to the body count or whatever), but there was not nearly enough feedback. Proposed citations were another source of comment, but these depended on the persistence of the initiating officer(s), and on their being afforded the time and data necessary to composition of a recommendation that would survive the sucessive levels of scrutiny to which these proposed awards were subjected.

Verdi provided selected mission summaries to his correspondent, from which I have further selected. (He was addressing missions specific to a campaign or campaigns the correspondent was researching, so many of the mission summaries prove his point of "hours of boredom.") I have ignored many of the summaries which contain no significant (to me) comment.

15 Sep 67
Event 48
VERDI/STIENON: 20mm gun, 4/M-117GP
KOTTULA/MEDORS: 7/M-117GP
EDDY/TREMPER: 7/M-117GP
Target: Scheduled Covey/Misty control, TOT 1745; Diverted Milky (MSQ) due to weather.*
BDA: None (no bombs dropped)
Remarks: Fiasco: Milky unable to receive APN-154 beacon; unable at target VFR due HEAVY rain north of DMZ; unable any radar IP due HEAVY rain (precipitation clutter flooded scope). Brought ordnance home, land below min fuel (GCA recovery DAG). Monsoon early this year (mission card thoroughly watermarked).

Note: See McCutcheon for brief account of USAF MSQ (Sky Spot). MSQ radar was more powerful than TPQ and was capable of tracking aircraft primary radar return (skin paint) under normal conditions. APN-154 beacon received TPQ radar frequency and replied with augmented return, facilitating acquisition and consistent tracking under all conditions: APN-154 did NOT receive MSQ radar frequency, and so we could not provide MSQ operators with augmented return necessary to acquire and track in bad weather (heavy precipitation). The converse was true (i.e. USAF aircraft carried beacons compatible with MSQ. The lesson? One more instance in which NAVAIRSYS-COM was more concerned with fighting AF than with fighting the enemy. Why were we diverted to MSQ rather than to TPQ on this sortie? Probably because TPQ's were saturated (with traffic as well as rain) or out for maintenance. BSQ's (and MSQ's) by themselves could not handle the numbers of airplanes which in-country tactical units could put in the air.

Author's note: Some of the acronyms and abbreviations may be arcane to the reader. Clarification: The pilot's name appears first, followed by that of his RIO. Names are followed by the armament carried on their airplane. Covey and Misty refer to FACs (Forward Air Controllers). In the case of Misty, a fast FAC, flying the F-100. Covey FACs flew slower O-1, O-2 and later, OV-10 aircraft. BDA refers to Bomb Damage Assessment. MSQ, TPQ refer to methods of dropping bombs under direction from ground radar stations.

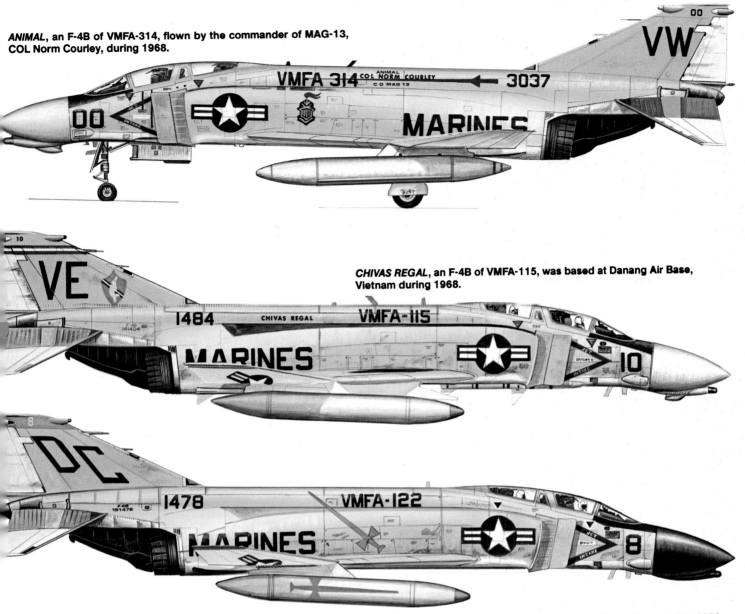

ANIMAL, an F-4B of VMFA-314, flown by the commander of MAG-13, COL Norm Courley, during 1968.

CHIVAS REGAL, an F-4B of VMFA-115, was based at Danang Air Base, Vietnam during 1968.

VMFA-122 Phantoms carried these unit markings during 1968.

A pair of VMFA-542 Phantoms parked in concrete revetments at Chu Lai. The soil at Chu Lai was primarily sand and required a thin layer of asphalt over the packed sand to support the aluminum planks which made up the ramps and runway. (McDonnell Douglas via Bob Pukala)

19 Sep 67
Event 47
VERDI/MEDORS: 7 X 4/5 ffar
McANNALLY/EASTMAN: 7 X 4/5 ffar
Target: YD-142796, artillery positions (scheduled alternate, TOT 0800)
BDA: Not observed
Remarks: Wrong ordnance; flight leader control, as COVEY not on station.

NOTE: Unless you get a secondary explosion, it is almost impossible to assess any sort of damage from a high-performance tactical airplane (even with two pairs of eyes), especially when the target is dug in (as most enemy targets in or near the DMZ were). The best that could be said in this instance was that for the 15 minutes that we worked over the target coordinates, nobody was manning (much less firing) any artillery pieces.

22 Sep 67
Event 43
VERDI/STEINON: 20mm gun, 4/CBU
BERGAN/SIMONE: 20mm gun, 4/CBU Target: No coordinate, no description (pre-briefed or post-briefed); TPQ, TOT 0930
BDA: Not reported
Remarks: Calibrated level release at 3000 AGL, 400 KTAS; NWL-107 fuze arm time 7.0 secs. Bearing in mind this was a daylight VMC TPQ mission, the following verbatim transcript of mission card is illuminating;
'Many orbits. Nobody briefed:
'Vector 200 at 3,000 ft toward 5,000 ft mountains!!
'Two break-locks, Bingo at 1000....PFUI!*
'Why are we in the business of OpEval-ing NWL-107??
'PISS ON 1st MAW!!"
NOTE: We landed below minimum fuel. Besides three obvious lessons (which you don't have to be an aviator to spot), there are a couple of further points; First, TPQ breaks lock at low altitudes (we already knew this, and did not need it demonstrated in Quang Tri Province); next, the same Wing Operations Section which put this idiotic event on the FRAGO were the people who raised righteous objections to innovations proposed by the troops best qualified to evaluate them, namely the tactical squadrons. Nobody on the ground got any benefit from this sortie.

25 Sep 67
Event 31
VERDI/STEINON: 4 X 19/2.75 ffar, 6/Mk 82 Snakeye
FRASER/HOLT: 12/Mk 82 Snakeye
Target: XD-704465 (scheduled/on call, Moray 14 Ground FAC control, TOT 1300)
BDA: By FAC: '100% coverage; one secondary explosion'.
Remarks: Six bomb runs, three rocket runs at minimum altitude in very tight terrain, 1308 - 1330. This was a textbook CAS mission....Good Show.

28 Sep 67
Event 33
VERDI/STEINON: 20mm gun, 4/M-117 GP
OSANTOWSKI/DEARING: 20mm gun, 4/M-117 GP
Target: YD-253773, mortar positions (scheduled TOT 1700, Red Marker 4 control).
BDA: 100/30; dest 2/bunkers, 1/structure.
Remarks: Actual TOT 1712 - 1718. As previously noted, M-117s were good for blast (clearing zones, destroying structures, killing enemy in contact), but they were not much good for digging (1) because of fat shape, and (2) because thinner case would fracture in hard ground (resulting in low order or dud).

9 Nov 67
Event 503
VERDI/STEINON: 20mm gun, 6/Mk 81 ldgp
DOUGAL/BARDON: 12 Mk 81 ldgp
Target: YD-125778, bunker complex (scheduled TOT 1715, Fingerprint 52 control)

BDA: 100/50; 'uncovered' 2 bunkers.
Remarks: Mk 81s were not much use for digging either (too small). Furthermore, mechanical nose fuzes (M-904) were instantaneous (nose fuzes with delay settings were unreliable, as the fuze could be destroyed before functioning, resulting in a dud...which, as noted in text, the enemy would then convert to a mine). Tail fuzes were electric (M-990), but not selectable; and you could not install both nose and tail fuzes (as you could with the old M-series fat bombs). Thanks, NWL!
Note on flight crews: IAW squadron SOP for flight operations, crew consisted of pilot/RIO TEAM, and our crews had been stabilized as of first weapons deployment Apr 67. Of course, everyone else said we couldn't sustain stabilized crews in combat (and the Wing's personnel "mixmaster" program was calculated to prove them right); but we did it just the same. The rule was a pilot flew with his RIO, and vice-versa; of course, there were substitutions for a variety of reasons more or less obvious...but these were the exception. My back-seater was Julian STIENON, AND FOR MOST OF MY F-4 missions, he flew with me.

13 Nov 67
Event 17
VERDI/STEINON: 9/Mk 82 ldgp (dc) ('daisy-cutter' fuze extensions)
Target: YD-104777, scheduled TPQ. TOT 0200
BDA: Not observed.
Remarks: Actual TOT 0154; if anyone was walking down the trail, those daisy-cutters would make instant hamburger.

29 Nov 67
Event 22
VERDI/STEINON: 20mm gun, 6/Mk 82 ldgp
OSANTOWSKI/DEARING: 12 Mk 82 ldgp
Target: YD-200793, bunker complex (scheduled on-call, Fingerprint 46 control, TOT 1730).
BDA: By FAC (A): 75% coverage, 65% destr: 4/bunkers, 3 structures destroyed.
Remarks: Gun stoppage before fire-out.

NOTE: Mk 11 20MM gun was mounted in Mk 4 gun pod containing 750 rounds, which was carried on center station. Loose Duece tactics were employed air-to-ground, which meant FAC had to be briefed concerning our "double attack" and had to consent to employment of gun or rockets against enemy ground fire simultaneously with principal attack against designated target. The idea was for 'bomber' to concentrate on target, while "the shotgun" suppressed AAA/AW fire. Sometimes (when FAC knew location of enemy AAA/AW, actual or probable; and/or when troops were in close contact with enemy) specific/restricted locations were assigned to "shotgun". Rarely, FAC/FAC(A) would object to this procedure (usually because he had never seen it before). It required more proficiency and more coordination, but it definitely succeeded in its purpose, which was to reduce hits by ground-fire on the airplanes. Also worthy of emphasis is that no incidents involving "short rounds" occurred.

5 Dec 67
Event 19
VERDI/FERGUSON: 20mm gun, 4/M-117 rgp (retarded M-117 tail donated by 366 TFW)
McENCROE/LEAR: 6 x 19/2.75 ffar, 6/Mk 81 rgp
Target: YD-175745, On-call Fingerprint 44 control.
BDA: '85%' was all we got out of the FAC(A)...but see Remarks.

Remarks: We waited an hour to get on this target while Super Grunts (Recon) sorted out with the FAC(A) exactly where all their troops were...the more careful operators not only wanted to account for everyone, they were also reluctant to tell too much on the radio (the bad guys listened). We didn't mind...we took on extra gas from our tanker 1358-1405, then worked over the *objective 1428 - 1435. This strike was, incidentally, first use by USMC aircraft of retarded M-117 (snakeye-type)...and excellent munition. The customer was as pleased as we were...a very good show.*

There were many more mission summaries in these papers that my space here does not allow me to reprint. There was also more amplifying comment on tactics and procedures which presumably will all come out when John Verdi writes his own book on the Vietnam War.

John Verdi was an unconventional Vietnam warrior; he wanted to win the war, and was willing to put his life on the line to do it. Perhaps more significantly, (and more sadly) he was willing to put his career on the line.

JACK McENCROE

...joined the Marine Corps during 1965. He earned his wings in December of 1966 and, after considerable effort, got into F-4s. Jack had wanted to fly the Phantom all along and one of his instructors had advised him that the best way to make sure he got what he wanted was to return from leave early, check in at his duty base and if they did not give him what he wanted, check back out on leave and return the next day. He had completed his flight training and was in San Diego, with orders to report to MCAS El Toro. On his initial visit to El Toro, he discovered that the officer in charge of flight assignments was a Marine helicopter pilot, who thought all Marine aviators should fly helicopters. The helicopter officer assigned Jack to helos no less than five times, resulting in five checkouts and returns. On the last attempt, the helo officer told Jack, "Look, Lieutenant, this is the Marine Corps and you will damn well go where I tell you!"

As he was walking out the door, a sympathetic warrant officer pulled him aside and said, "Come back in thirty minutes and we'll see what we can do for you." When he returned, the helo officer was not around and the warrant officer sent him over to MAG 33, the F-4 group. Jack had told him that he wanted to go to the squadron with the most F-4s and the fewest pilots. When he reported to the group commander, the CO said, "Well, I see you want to be a photo pilot?" Jack said, "No sir." "But," said the C.O., "We got you in the squadron with the most F-4s and the fewest pilots!" Jack repeated that he did not want to go to a reconnaissance squadron and the CO said that he had one slot left in VMFA-122, which was scheduled to deploy to Vietnam in six months. Jack jumped at the chance. He was a second lieutenant and destined to remain so for longer than necessary. His promotion papers had followed him out of flight school, and were sitting on the helo officer's desk, ready to be served. Jack, fearing that he could lose his F-4 assignment if he returned to pick up his promotion papers, decided to wait for the papers to catch up with him at their own bureaucratic speed. This is his narrative of his Vietnam experience:

VMFA-122 Trans-Paced their own airplanes, deploying to Vietnam as a squadron. (This only happened early in the war. Later, those units in the war zone generally stayed...in name only. The personnel changed as the thirteen month tour requirement caused a constant turn-over.) It took us about six days to complete the move. Four of us made it to Hawaii the first day, but the balance of the squadron had join-up and refueling problems and it took them three days to finally get there. We jumped off the next day for Wake Island, then to Guam, the Philippines, and on into Danang. We were doing a division takeoff from Wake when my left main tire blew. Fortunately, I was on the left wing of the lead airplane, so when I went careening off into the weeds, we didn't collide. I hollered for my RIO, Steve Lear, to hang on, telling him that I thought we might be going into the water. Tongue in cheek, heart in throat, he said, "I'm right behind you mane!" (His Cajun accent turned 'man' into 'mane.')

A few years previous, an Air Force C-135 had caught fire on takeoff and even though the pilots successfully aborted the

Jack McEncroe (kneeling) and Steve Lear preflight the nose gear of their Phantom during VMFA-122 workups at El Toro, California, prior to their deployment to Vietnam. (McEncroe)

takeoff, the fire trucks could not get to them in time to prevent their dying in the fire. As a result of that crash, Wake routinely had the fire trucks chase all flights down the runway, or had them stationed at the departure end. When we headed off into the weeds, the fire trucks were hot on our tail. The friction of the wheel, sans tire, on concrete and coral had started a fire in the left main gear, freezing the brakes. As we were approaching the water, we slid across an old World War II runway that was parallel to the end of the duty runway. I literally bent my right rudder pedal; I kicked it so hard trying to turn on that old runway. The force of my kick freed up the brakes and we did a smart right turn and slid to a stop right on the end of the duty runway. Steve hollered, "I'm getting out of here!" Well, I knew that fire truck was in hot pursuit and would probably cover us with foam to smother any incipient fire real quick. I told him not to leave just yet, but it was too late...he had already unplugged his headset. He opened his canopy just in time to be turned into a snow cone by the predictable blast of foam from the fire truck. I had to laugh!

VMFA-122 was a unique squadron in many ways. The men, the mission, the camraderie and the leadership molded a great bunch of guys into a very efficient and proud unit. We were John Verdi's Marines and proud of it! We were the only Marine Corps F-4 squadron with all-weather capability. We flew with up radars and up weapons delivery systems. We had originally

McEncroe and Everett sitting on 750 pound bombs on a bomb trailer at Danang. McEncroe went to VMFA-115 as a check pilot after his initial combat tour with VMFA-122. (McEncroe)

27

This freshly painted overall Black sharkmouthed F-4B at Danang still has masking tape covering the canopy and air intakes. The purpose for the overall Black paint scheme is unknown. (Norm Taylor)

RM 22, an RF-4B of VMCJ-1, on final approach for landing at an airbase in Vietnam. The Marines were the only service to operate the RF-4B. (McDonnell Douglas)

A Marine Corps Phantom pilot with Khaki flight suit under his G suit survival vest. The Khaki flight suit was eventually superseded by Green Nomex suit.

An RF-4B of VMCJ-1. This squadron spent more consecutive time in war zone than any other Marine squadron (1965-70).

An F-4B of VMFA-542 rolls in on a Viet Cong target during 1966. Marine Phantom units were used primarly in the air-to-ground role.

29

McEncroe and his RIO, Steve Lear, in the cockpit of their Phantom before a mission over South Vietnam. (McEncroe)

been scheduled to deploy aboard the USS RANGER (CVA-61) for carrier qualifications. Then the communists attacked the air base at Danang and blew up two fighter squadrons and our assignment was changed. We arrived at Danang during August of 1967. We flew close air support, high angle dives, and TPQs, which I thought were a waste of time...someone trying to up the tonnage of bombs dropped. We escorted the A-6s up into the Hanoi-Haiphong areas of North Vietnam. We also flew a lot in northern Laos and it is one of those missions which stands out in my mind. I was not on this mission, but it occurred on the day I flew the most missions of my tour.

John Drew was the first replacement pilot to arrive in the squadron and we really never got a chance to get to know him very well. Naturally, the rest of us were very tight, having gone through F-4 combat training together and then deploying as a unit to Vietnam. On the hot pad the night before his sixth mission, I got to talking to John. He had been a couple of months ahead of me in the training command, but had been assigned to the east coast. When he joined our squadron, being a new guy, he was suspect in a very protective environment. We were all very proud of being in VMFA-122 and threatened by anyone who might tarnish our record. John was scheduled to fly the next day, and oh, how he embellished, rather than tarnished our image!

On that day, Steve Lear and I had flown two missions and were scheduled to fly an A-6 escort to Hanoi. It had been an eventful day even before the mission to Hanoi. Bob Hope's USO group was on base and Gary Fors and I had gotten front-row seats because we had to fly a mission immediately after the show. Gary was killed on that mission. Gary was to be the only original member of John Verdi's VMFA-122 who did not come home. He was a great guy!

I flew my escort mission to Hanoi that night. Our usual method of operation was for the A-6s to take the eastern route to Hanoi, over the Gulf of Tonkin, then turn in somewhere south of Haiphong. We would take the western route, up over Laos, then cross into North Vietnam and hold about 14 miles west of Hanoi, at 14,000 feet in a figure eight holding pattern. Twice the North Vietnamese had launched MIGs against us. I chased one MIG towards Red China, but could not convince Red Crown (the radar controller for North Vietnam, stationed off the coast in a cruiser) to give us permission to fire. The rules of engagement at that time specified that we had to make visual identification before firing on any aircraft. We figured that was ridiculous, since we were the only airplanes up there except for Air Force recce airplanes, and their positions were known.

The only ECM we had was chaff strips carried in our speed brake wells...which was the same as not having anything, since I don't know anybody crazy enough to pop their speed brakes over Hanoi! They only fired two SAMs at me that night, but the triple-A was spectacular! I always thought they used the SAMs like a cow-puncher...trying to herd us into flak traps, where they might have everything from 37MM to 100MM AAA. AAA fired at night never failed to get your attention!

The A-6s would come across at low level to drop their ordnance. There was never any doubt about where they were, because the AAA and tracers chasing them were very visible. They would then head out with us doing figure eights to cover them and ourselves on the way out. We got down to Udorn, Thailand, refueled and headed back to Hanoi to escort the next group of A-6s. After they were clear, we refueled again at Udorn, then headed down into the valley that Gary Fors had been shot down in. We had gotten his RIO, Guy Lashlee, who evaded hundreds of NVA for two hours, but there was no sign of Gary and we never found him.

That made four missions that day and I was beat when I got back to Danang. I was heading for my hooch when the Executive Officer, "Bear" Waldvogel, came running up and said, "John Drew has just been shot up! Can you take my hop?" (John Verdi was on R&R, so Bear was the acting CO and needed to be at squadron operations.)

John's mission had been up around Tchepone in northern Laos. This was a hotly contested area and you could always expect to get a rousing welcome when you went up there. As he was pulling off the target after his first run, he took a hit. The 50 caliber tracer round came through the left side of the airplane, blew off the top of the throttles, went through his left shoulder and the top of the ejection seat, and spent itself on the canopy. A fragment of this round caused the ejection light to go on. Bill Simone was John's backseater and even though the light was on and the cockpit was smoky, he sensed that this was not the place to eject if you could help it. He asked John if they should eject, but John was not able to answer...yet. Bill could tell John had been hit, since there was blood and bits of flesh all over the cockpit. On his second try, Bill got an answer out of his pilot. The airplane was under control and John told Bill not to eject yet. He would try for a safer area before they punched out.

With the airplane under control, and his leader, Jacques Naviaux, talking to the Search and Rescue people, John's main concern was in staying conscious. He was losing blood, and after struggling with his survival vest and getting a compress out, he dropped it on the floor of the cockpit, out of reach. (As it turned out, the size of the wound was so large that the compress would not have helped much anyway.) Once over the coast, John made the decision to try for Danang, 70 miles south. Bill kept up a steady stream of conversation and encouragement. At thirty miles out, Lead called for the morest arresting gear to be set, since he didn't know how much control Drew would have over landing speed. Drew was flying with his right hand only...the left was lying useless in his lap....which meant that he had to reach over and make throttle adjustments with his right hand, using what was left of the throttles. The landing was routine. As soon as they stopped, Simone climbed out, inserted the safety pins in both seats and helped the medics get Drew out of the airplane. He went into immediate surgery, and was evacuated the next day. John Drew had proved that he belonged in VMFA-122. He was awarded the Silver Star and Bill Simone was awarded the Distinguished Flying Cross.

My next mission, which was my fifth of that day, was against the guns that had shot Drew. We got those guns. Since I was fly-

This armament load was used by VMFA-122 on short close air support missions (there are no external fuel tanks). The three 20MM Vulcan cannon pods could wreak havoc with the enemy when all three were fired simultaneously.

A VMFA-122 Phantom loaded with six 500 pound Snakeyes on the inboard wing stations and napalm bombs on the centerline station. VMFA-122 regularly flew missions deep into North Vietnam as MIGCAP for Marine A-6 strikes against Hanoi-Haiphong. Their Phantoms were fitted with tail-warning radar and ECM equipment for these missions. (USMC)

McEncroe and Lear airborne in their VMFA-323 Phantom during March of 1968, at the height of the battle for Khe Sanh. The battle was one of the most lopsided victories in history, resulting in the loss of three full divisions of NVA troops. This loss set back the communist plan for an invasion of South Vietnam by four years. (McEncroe)

ing Bear's hop, Steve Lear was not with me on this mission, but another great RIO, J. Steinon, was. We arrived overhead Tchepone and the place lit up! We put them out of business on the first run. It was a great feeling!

Steve Lear and I had perfected a rather unique bomb delivery ....one which just about guaranteed good results, and we never got hit by ground fire while using it, although there was plenty of it around! My delivery consisted of rolling inverted, then pulling into a 90 degree dive, which gave me the option of rolling the airplane to any position necessary to keep the pipper on the target. We never had to worry about exact mil settings on the bombsight, because we knew the bomb was pretty much going where we aimed it. The hairy part, for Steve, was the pull-out after dropping. We would drop at 10,000 feet, then pull! The F-4 was text book limited to 7 or 8.5 Gs, but I figure we pulled 10 or 11 every time. It was tough on Steve, heading straight down at 600 knots with no control over the outcome, and tough on the airplane, but like I said, we hit the target and we never got hit ourselves using this delivery. In 352 combat missions, totaling 800 hours, we were only hit twice, both times on close air support missions where we were forced to use a flatter delivery trajectory.

The 1968 Tet Offensive provided us with some of the most challenging flying of the whole tour. Most of it was close air support, often operating under 400 foot ceilings. We dropped napalm at 600 knots and 25 feet and snakeye bombs at 600 knots and 100 feet. When you are doing that, then pulling 7 Gs coming off the target and trying to stay under that 400 foot ceiling...you are busy! It was also during this period that we began to see a more direct correlation between the bombing pauses that Lyndon Johnson mandated and the level of NVA activity in the south. After the Christmas bombing pause we got our butts blown away on 3 January, then again on the 29th and 30th. It was real clear to us that as long as we kept the pressure on them, we were winning the war. As soon as we gave them some breathing room, they would resupply and come after us again. Why wasn't it

obvious to Washington??!!

Most observers credit airpower and the gutty performance of the Marine grunts on the ground with winning the battle of Khe Sanh and they are right, but not for the reason most think. The Bubonic Plague gets a large assist for winning the battle of Khe Sanh. After we had shut off all supplies to the North Vietnamese armies around Khe Sanh, they resorted to killing and eating rats. When it was all over and we went into the jungles around Khe Sanh, we found mass graves for the victims of the plague. The war was over in March of 1968, then Johnson's bombing halt gave the enemy a chance to regroup. Prior to that time, we had pretty well pounded him into submission. In fact, in January I rarely saw a SAM fired in Route Pack Six and never down south, but after the bombing halt, we saw SAMs fired in Route Pack One! Lyndon Johnson was my Commander in Chief. The office I respected, the man I did not!

I left VMFA-122 at the end of January and transferred to VMFA-323 for a short time, then wound up my tour at Chu Lai as the squadron check pilot for MAG-13, where I gave all the new guys their first five rides and dodged numerous rocket attacks.

Flying the F-4 in defense of our country was very fulfilling and a tremendous thrill, yet those of us in the air were only an extension of our support people. The Marines in our maintenance shops were the finest men it has ever been my pleasure to know and they share in all our our successes. The F-4 was teamwork, and we were a great team! John Verdi's Marines......BURNER NOW!!

Jack resigned from the Marine Corps shortly after returning to the States and went to work for Delta Airlines. After numerous shoulder operations grounded him, he devoted all of his time to his real estate investment company. He lives in Steamboat Springs, Colorado, with his wife Anita and three daughters, Kelly, Katie, and Kristi.

Flying combat missions day in and day out created lots of opportunities for interesting incidents, such as this runaway Phantom. Crash crews survey the damage to the tail section amid the fire fighting foam which had been sprayed on the aircraft to prevent a fire. (McEncroe)

The Phantom was ultimately stopped when it punched its nose through the wall of a revetment. The boxes surrounding the F-4 are empty 20mm ammunition boxes. (McEncroe)

This F-4B of VMFA-122 was assigned to Jack McEncroe and Steve Lear. VMFA-122 was the only unit to employ three 20mm gun pods as a standard armament configuration.

Manny Simpson's night IFR close air support mission. According to Manny, "If you really want to know how dark it was, turn off the lights and look at this picture in moonlight!"

An F-4B Phantom of VMFA-323.

33

DONN BEATTY

Donn Beatty was in Naval Aviation Cadet training class 16-56. He received his commission and wings in June of 1957 and his first assignment was with VMF-312 at MCAS Beaufort, S.C., flying the North American FJ Fury. His next assignment followed graduation from Naval Intelligence School. He was assigned to MAG-32 as an S-2 Officer until February of 1960, when he joined 2nd ANGLICO in Camp Lejuene, North Carolina. After an interesting tour of duty at Guantanamo Bay, Cuba, he was assigned to training command as an Instructor Pilot in the TF-9 jet trainer at Beeville, Texas.

Following that assignment, he attended Naval Aviation Safety School at the University of Southern California. He was then assigned to MAG-11 at NAS Atsugi, Japan, as Group Safety Officer. He returned to MCAS El Toro, California in September of 1964, joining VMF(AW)-312 which had transitioned to the F-8 Crusader. The following February he transferred to VMF(AW)-122. In July of 1966 he was assigned to the 3rd MAW staff as Wing Special Services Officer. In January of 1967 he was reassigned to VMFA-122 which transitioned to the F-4B Phantom.

During the months preceding the TRANSPAC to Vietnam, VMFA-122 practiced night navigation through the mountains to the various bombing ranges, using the F-4's radar. They also practiced loft bombing and radar bombing. The practice using the Phantom's weapons system radar for ground mapping navigation would prove to be very helpful when they got to Vietnam. Donn recalled at least two occasions where GCA controllers nearly steered him into mountains on the approach to Danang. After that, he said, "We did all of our own self-contained approaches, using the F-4's radar." The use of the radar for this approach was unique to VMFA-122. It was one of many unique characteristics of this squadron, which was led by one of the most brilliant mavericks in Southeast Asia.

John Verdi was a commander who had his eye squarely on the mission. He had no use for careerists...the "ticket punchers" who only did a Vietnam tour to enhance their military resume. Verdi encouraged innovation and never asked his troops to do something he would not do or had not done himself. Donn Beatty was his Maintenance Officer and, as such, was responsible for many of the armament and navigation modifications done to VMFA-122 airplanes. His account of the tour is an adventure, or a horror story, depending on your point of view. Donn said he enjoyed it. These are his reminiscences:

Working for John Verdi made the tour that much more colorful. I remember one time when he sent me what we called a "blue blazer"... a strongly worded message, written on blue notepaper, that indicated that he was not happy with maintenance and that if it didn't improve by Tuesday, he would take it over himself. I sat down and wrote him a fifteen page, typed, single space reply, which he sat on for two weeks before ack-

Plane Captain CPL Lonnie Wright with Donn Beatty next to "their" Phantom on the line at Danang, Vietnam. The plane captain was responsible for seeing that the aircraft was mission ready at all times. (Donn Beatty)

nowledging it...but he left me alone after that. He would really respect you if you stood up for your beliefs. He was a real warrior, who was in his element in combat and he had no respect for any commander who he thought wasn't. He declared the theater commander persona non-grata in the squadron and would not publicly acknowledge any orders from him. This caused the rest of us to do some fancy scrambling to forestall a showdown. On two occasions, I got him to do something that no one else could, which was to apologize to the entire squadron in formation for some of his actions. The second time he told me, "This is the second time I have done this and don't ever expect me to do it again...no matter what I do!"

The Transpac to Vietnam was an adventure in itself. As Maintenance Officer, I was responsible for making sure that the airplanes were ready for the long, over water flight. On the days preceding the flight, the squadron pilots began to get real picky about their airplanes. It seemed like if eight planes went out, four would come back with maintenance gripes. If six went out, three would come back, etc. etc. Finally, I asked for a full day for maintenance, then told the pilots that when we left, if I saw any of them turn back, I would ram them! We got seventeen airplanes to Hawaii that day! Our next leg was on to Wake Island. We got there just ahead of a typhoon. No one wanted to stick around for that, so we hustled out of there the next day. As Maintenance Officer, I was always scheduled to fly the sickest airplane. On this flight, that happened to be an airplane with a hole in one flap, which had been put there by an air hose that broke loose from the APU during start. We couldn't go with a hole in the flap, so we rushed across the field to a Pan American Airways maintenance facility to see if they could help us. They gave us a roll of "speedy tape", a tape that resembles duct tape, but which will hold up at high speed. I liked that stuff so much that I got a few more rolls from them. That speed tape saved us from having to go to major repairs in the combat zone many times when a bullet hole in a flap or tail or some non-vital spot had to be repaired before we could fly.

Our next stop was Agana, on Guam. From there we would go direct to Subic Bay, then on to Danang. I was in the last flight to leave Agana, flying number four in the sick bird. Don "Bear" Waldvogel, our Executive Officer, was leading the flight. As Bear got up to rotation speed, he blew a tire on one of his mains. He wasn't going fast enough to get airborne, and the Phantom was loaded with all the fuel it could carry. I watched him veer off the runway and head across the airport, with the airplane shedding pieces as he went. There was a tremendous cloud of dirt, airplane pieces, and assorted crap flying as the Phantom headed straight for the Pan Am terminal. The wing tanks ruptured, and the airplane was now trailing flames as it jumped one of the jet blast deflectors and finally came to rest on top of a Volkswagen right in front of the terminal coffee shop, scaring the hell out of the customers.

Waldvogel and his RIO blew the canopies off, and the RIO

Donn Beatty in the cockpit of his Phantom at Danang after returning from a mission. His Phantom carries a Black tank marking on the intake plate indicating one kill over an NVA tank. (Beatty)

calmly stepped out. Don was pumping so much adrenalin though, that as he grabbed the canopy frame and pulled himself up and out of the airplane, he did a complete somersault over the nose, landing on his head and knocking himself silly. The fire and rescue squad was there quickly and they dragged him away from the wreckage, scratching his knee and giving him the only injury he received from this escapade. They loaded him into the ambulance and headed for the flight line. We had taxied back, of course and as the ambulance approached the flight line, I steeled myself to get the bad news. When the ambulance stopped, the Bear staggered out with a cheerful, "Hi, Donn!" We left for Danang the next day.

Our radar modification allowed us to pick up a radar beacon placed at the end of the runway. That was the secret to our self-contained approach and I believe we were the only squadron who did that. Since we often flew at maximum gross weight, or higher, I also modified the jettison switch in the airplane to make it easier to reach. I also installed an old ARN-6 loop antenna in one airplane in order to be able to pick up and home in on Hanoi radio when we went to Route Pack Six.

At the request of the CO, I went out and tried some 30 degree dive bombing with 500 pound Snakeye bombs. These were unsuccessful because we just didn't have enough depression on the gunsight and the delivery speeds were too slow for safe maneuvering. After nearly making grass stains on the entire body of my F-4, I recommended to Verdi that we not pursue this idea further. But this was an indication of how we were always looking for more effective ways to fight the war. We also installed wiring which would allow us to hang the 20MM Vulcan cannon pods on the outboard wing stations (the F-4B/J Phantom could only carry the gun pods on the centerline station.) Unfortunately, the gun pods were so unreliable that you could never be assured that they would all fire at the same time. When they didn't, the assymetrical recoil made it tough to hit anything...but when they did, it was some experience! The recoil felt like you were actually backing up! All of these special missions were in addition to our regularly assigned missions.

We often got attacked by Viet Cong or NVA troops, who would lob mortars or rockets onto the airport. One revetment in particular seemed to take more than its share of punishment. The airport crash-fire-rescue unit was on the other side of the field and, since it was an Air Force unit, their first priority was usually the USAF. That meant that if both sides got hit and airplanes were burning in both locations, theirs got saved and ours didn't. There was also a salvage dump on the Air Force side of the field and one day while I was reconnoitering I spotted what appeared to be a derelict water truck. I sent one of my staff NCOs over to see if he could talk the Air Force out of the old truck. He did, and managed to get it running. We took that old beat-up truck and installed a 55 gallon drum of dry chemical fire suppressant on the back. With the combination of water and chemical, we fabricated a foam generator and we were able to save three airplanes which would have been lost in subsequent attacks. Our little 'scrounged-up' fire department became so popular that we actually sold it to the incoming squadron when we left to rotate home.

"Little John" Cummings was my RIO during my tour. He later returned to Vietnam and with his pilot, Tom "Bear" Lasseter, shot down a MiG-21. It was the only kill by a Marine squadron during the war. One night Little John and I were up north, flying MIGCAP for the A-6s. We were in a holding pattern over Yen Bai and, as the A-6s started out after their bomb runs, we picked up a target heading their way. It was a sucker target and as soon as we turned on it, the MiG did a one-eighty and headed for the middle of Hanoi, trying to draw us into a SAM and flak trap. I got fixated on that target, chasing him in burner, trying to catch him before he got to Hanoi. Suddenly I realized that I should be watching my fuel. I looked down and, sure enough, we were beyond bingo fuel. There was no way we were going to get to the MiG, so I headed west for our refueling point, near Udorn. After

A crowd of Marines survey the damage to this burned out F-4 which was one of the casualties of a North Vietnamese Army rocket attack on Danang. (Beatty)

figuring the fuel, I realized we weren't even going to make Udorn. I started calling for a tanker to come out and meet us. Thank God there was one on station, and we got to him and plugged in with 800 pounds of fuel showing on the totalizer. It was 0400, dark, and we had flown a long night mission, but I made one of the sweetest plug-ins on that tanker of my entire career.

Most of our missions north were MIGCAP missions for the Marine Attack squadrons taking part in Rolling Thunder and most of them that I flew were at night. One of the few day missions that I recall was led by John Verdi. There was supposed to be four of us escorting 'Willie the Whale,' the EF-10 Skyknight electronic warfare airplane, which was headed for Haiphong on an intelligence gathering mission. I was flying number three, with Jack McEncroe on Verdi's wing. My wingman developed hydraulic problems and had to turn back, but I kept going. When we got to our station, we started a high station weave over the EF-10. Within a couple of minutes we picked up a target to the south and Verdi and McEncroe took off after the MIG, leaving me as the sole protector of the ECM bird as he trolled for enemy radar emissions. The implications of this sunk in in a big hurry. There I was, all alone, over Haiphong Harbor in broad daylight, with China close at hand. I was sure they would start shooting missiles and send MiGs up to try to shoot us down. I was surprised when they didn't. Eventually, Verdi and McEncroe returned when their contact turned out to be a friendly and we headed home. There was one final bit of drama as we egressed. I looked back and down at our seven o'clock and spotted two airplanes low, down on the water. I called bogies and you never saw three airplanes reverse so fast! We were armed and ready to shoot when we identified an F-8 and A-4...playing games where they shouldn't have been.

Warrant Officer J.O. Thornton, Donn Beatty, R.S. Brown, and John Cummings inspect the bomb load on Beatty's Phantom. The mission set a new record for the squadron — 10,000 tons of bombs dropped by VMFA-122. (Beatty)

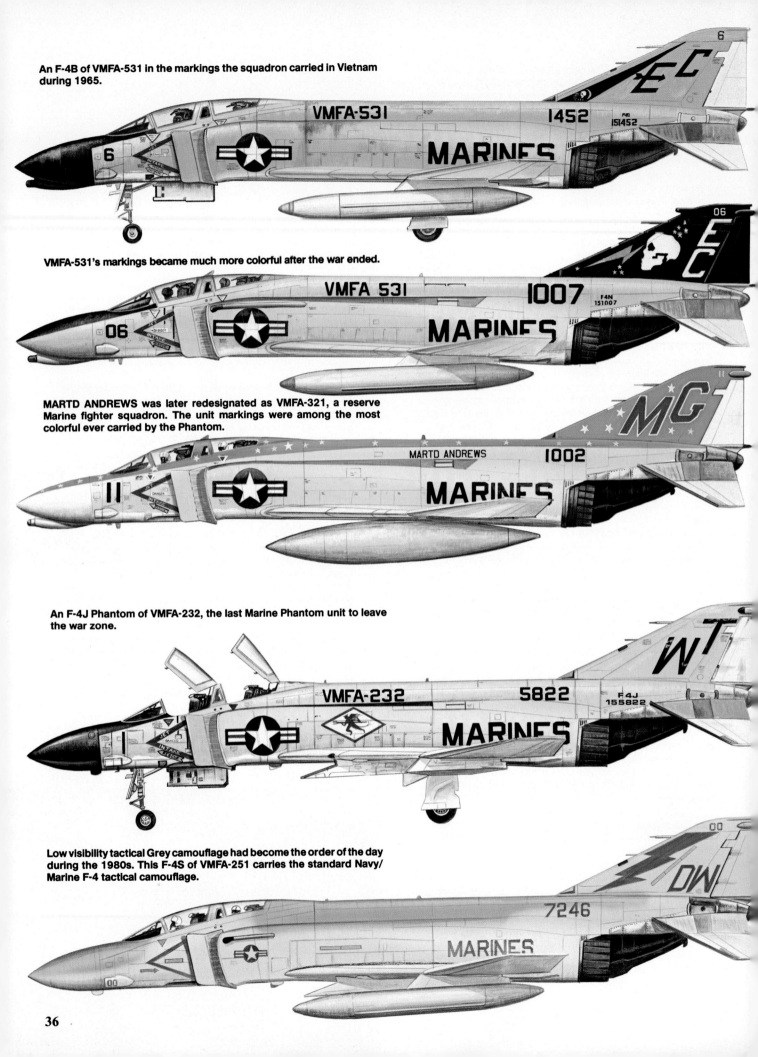

An F-4B of VMFA-531 in the markings the squadron carried in Vietnam during 1965.

VMFA-531's markings became much more colorful after the war ended.

MARTD ANDREWS was later redesignated as VMFA-321, a reserve Marine fighter squadron. The unit markings were among the most colorful ever carried by the Phantom.

An F-4J Phantom of VMFA-232, the last Marine Phantom unit to leave the war zone.

Low visibility tactical Grey camouflage had become the order of the day during the 1980s. This F-4S of VMFA-251 carries the standard Navy/Marine F-4 tactical camouflage.

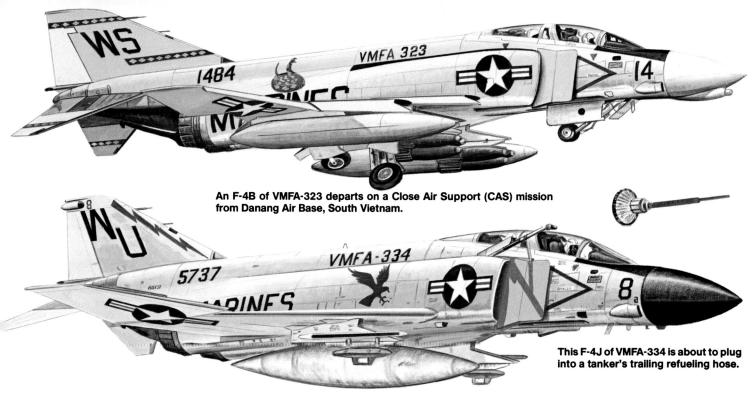

An F-4B of VMFA-323 departs on a Close Air Support (CAS) mission from Danang Air Base, South Vietnam.

This F-4J of VMFA-334 is about to plug into a tanker's trailing refueling hose.

An F-4J of VMFA-232 on the ramp at Osan Air Base, South Korea, during June of 1974. VMFA-232 was one of the more colorful Marine Phantom units. (Norm Taylor)

(Left) A VMFA-323 crew about to board their Phantom for a mission over South Vietnam. The F-4 is loaded with Snakeye retarded bombs, weapons well suited for CAS missions. The pilot wears a camouflage flight suit, while the RIO wears a Tan flight suit. (McEncroe)

(Below) Checker tailed F-4Bs of VMFA-312 parked on the flight line at MCAS Beaufort, South Carolina, on 12 April 1966. (Norman E. Taylor)

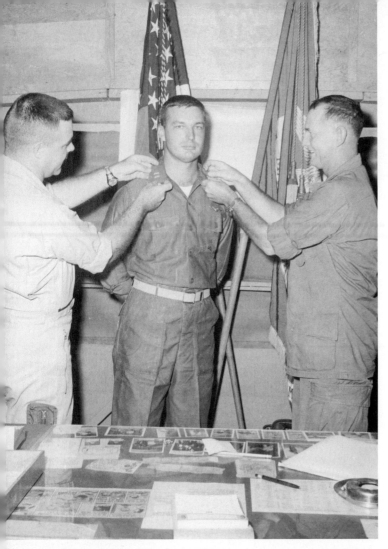

MAJ Donn Beatty receives his Oak Leaves by the commander who followed John Verdi as skipper of VMFA-122 in Vietnam. (Beatty)

On my first 100 missions, I never got hit. On my last 229 it seemed like I got hit every time I went out. Of course, many of those missions were close air support and I had the habit of dueling with quad fifties (actually quad-mounted 12.7MM machine guns.) While several of them were silenced, I never took what could be considered a serious hit. But on one mission in the Khe Sanh area, during the siege, we were called in to blast one of those quad fifties, which had just nailed one of our A-4s. I had six pods of 2.75 inch rockets and I let them all go right on top of that gun position. After I pulled off, the FAC said, "Well, he's either chained to the gun and dead, or he jumped in a spider hole when he saw you coming and is back out again." I said, "There's only one way to find out!", and rolled in on him again. Trouble is, I didn't have any ordnance, and that guy had been in a hole, because he really filled the sky with lead! While we never did get him, I believe I ran him out of ammunition, scared hell out of my wingman...and on later speculation...me too!

The most satisfying missions were close air support missions where you knew you had saved somebody's butt. I recall one where we had troops in contact and I was loaded with napalm. After we had made multiple passes and pulled off, the guy on the ground called to thank us, and I could hear the troops in the background yelling and cheering. That sent chills up my spine.

One innovative mission that we worked on was radar loft bombing. There was an island off the coast, near Dong Ha, named Tiger Island, which everyone assumed was deserted. We used it as a target to perfect our technique. When we got pretty good and started to get some hits, we began taking fire. Here the place had been occupied the whole time and we thought we were flying practice missions! By the time they started shooting at us though, we were good enough to hit them, and we soon silenced those guns.

Donn flew his 329 combat missions in less than eleven flying months. When he returned from Southeast Asia he was assigned to the Marine Air Weapons Training Unit, Pacific. He was responsible for the F-4 air-to-ground and air-to-air weapons tactics development. He attended USAF Fighter Weapons School and advised the Navy on formation of its now-famous air-to-air fighter school, Top Gun. After his tour at MAWTU, he attended Auburn University to finish his degree; then, was assigned to MCAS Beaufort, as Executive Officer of VMFA-451, which he later commanded for fifteen months. From there it was on to MCAS Iwakuni, Japan, on the Wing Staff. After that he was sent to Headquarters, Marine Corps in Washington. He retired from the Marine Corps during 1976 and today is Assistant Director of Transportation at DFW airport, in Dallas, Texas.

The HUMMER was a Marine Corps Douglas R4D Skytrain which was used as an intra-theatre transport. The old Skytrain operated out of Danang during August of 1968. (McEncroe)

During one North Vietnamese rocket attack, one of the 122MM B-40 rockets fired by the NVA blew a gaping hole through the VMFA-122 hangar wall. (McEncroe).

Jack McEncroe and his RIO, Steve Lear, pose with their Phantom prior to a mission with VMFA-323. The Phantom's ordnance load includes Zuni rockets, 500 pound Snakeye bombs, and napalm bombs. (McEncroe)

A VMFA-115 Phantom on the ramp at Ubon RTAFB, Thailand. The Phantom pilot landed at Ubon for fuel after a mission over Laos during 1968. The aircraft in the background are RTAF T-28 fighter-bombers. (Al Piccirillo via Norm Taylor)

These VMFA-115 F-4Bs are lightly loaded during a mission flown on 26 April 1966. The bomb shortage was a fact of operations faced by the Marines until late 1966 and early 1967. (USMC)

This VFMA-115 Phantom was loaded with four shot Zuni rocket pods on the centerline station and WW II vintage fat bombs on the inboard wing stations on 2 May 1966. Within two weeks an abortive coup would be staged in Danang which would require Air Marshall Ky to fly in 1,000 South Vietnamese Marines to restore order. (USMC)

This VMFA-115 Phantom at Nakhon Phanom RTAB, Thailand, has the nose radome opened to expose the radar for maintenance. (via John Santucci)

Jack McEncroe climbs aboard his VMFA-323 F-4B for a close air support (CAS) mission during July of 1968, while the unit was based at Danang Air Base, South Vietnam. (McEncroe)

VMFA-321, a Marine reserve squadron, celebrated the U.S. Bicentennial with these colorful markings. (Jim Sullivan)

Marine Captain Roy Stafford designed the Bicentennial paint scheme used on this VMFP-3 RF-4B. (McDonnell Douglas by Harry Gann)

Marine Corps tactical camouflage, like the Navy and Air Force, has evolved to shades of Gray. The tactical camouflage is designed to make the F-4 less visible in the air-to-air role. (Norm Taylor)

(Above) The pilots and RIOs of VMFA-115 pose with one of their Phantoms at Chu Lai during September of 1968. Jack McEncroe is fourth from the left, in a light colored flight suit. (McEncroe)

(Below) *CHIVAS REGAL*, an F-4B of VMFA-115, returns to Danang after a mission over Vietnam during 1971. The US pullout had begun and the North Vietnamese were building up for the Easter invasion of 1972. During this time more AAA sites were moved into South Vietnam and SAM batteries were positioned just across the DMZ. (USMC)

(Below) It was not uncommon for the Marines to take advantage of the hospitality of the USAF's 8th Tactical Fighter Wing at Ubon for fuel when a tanker was not available and landing at an alternate base became necessary. (Al Piccirillo via Norm Taylor)

F-4B Phantoms of VMFA-115 on the ramp at NAS Atsugi, Japan, during 1973. The Phantoms of the Silver Eagles had a distinctive White tail; with Red, White, and Blue stripes and the Silver eagle. (Norm Taylor)

BOB DOUGAL

Bob Dougal graduated from the U.S. Naval Academy during 1964. He hadn't planned to join the Marines, but during finals week at the Naval Academy the graduating class is asked to make their duty selection. Dougal had opted for Naval Aviation, hoping to play football at Pensacola and he got in line for that assignment. The Midshipmen were lined up according to class standing and his standing was so low that he was well back in the line. When he finally got to the front of the line, the officer in charge said, "I don't know anything about you playing football, but you are assigned to a flight school class beginning next January." (His class standing also meant that he couldn't get into flight school right away and would have to remain at the Naval Academy until January.) He said, "I'm not going to do that!" took his card back from the assignments officer and looked for another line to get into. The shortest line was for the Marines.

He went straight to Marine Corps boot camp, then on to flight school, receiving his wings in June of 1966. Flight school seemed to be a much better motivator than Annapolis and Bob finished high enough in his class to get a jet assignment. But his troubles with assignment officers were not over.

Bob and a fellow native of Washington state, Gary Fors, both got their wings on the same day and both checked in at the MCAS El Toro, California, personnel office at the same time. The Personnel Officer told them that they were going to fly C-130s. Gary was very outspoken, while Bob describes himself as "mild-mannered...at least, in the short run." The Personnel Officer was a major. Gary and Bob were first lieutenants. Under these circumstances, you would expect the Marines to get two new C-130 pilots. But Gary stood his ground and said, "We're not flying C-130s!" "Yes, you are!" "The hell we are!" Bob was sure they were headed for the brig. "You two are going to have to go over to the C-130 squadron!" "Nope, we're not going." The major relented...a little. "O.K., siddown over there. I'm going to lunch and I'll talk to you when I get back."

When the major returned, he told them that he had thought about it and decided that one of them could fly F-4s, but that one of then was going to HAVE to go to C-130s. Gary replied, "Nope, neither one of us is going to fly C-130s!" "My quota says one of you has to go!" "Tough shit! Neither one of us is going to fly C-130s!" After three hours of wrangling, the major finally said, "Alright, dammit! Both of you get the hell out of here and report to VMFA-122!" Bob figures the next fifteen guys didn't even get a chance to see that soft-hearted major...they just ended up with four throttles in their right hand. Bob's narrative of his tour with VMFA-122 follows:

When I reported into the squadron, Major Bob Hudson was the squadron commander. He was a very junior Major, which struck me as odd, since I figured command of an F-4 squadron would be considered a choice assignment. But we were a stateside squadron and all the new airplanes and spare parts were going to the airplanes in the combat zone. Hudson had been given command of a squadron of down airplanes, without spare parts. That created severe morale problems, but he was a good squadron commander and today is a Lieutenant General.

The only pilots who were getting any flying time to speak of were those who had received their orders to go to Southeast Asia. Morale was low because the squadron was not training as a unit and was really nothing more than a replacement depot for the combat squadrons. That all changed when the squadron was frozen and began training to go into combat as a unit. We began to receive priority in spare parts and in allocations of flying time. We also got a new squadron commander.

LTCOL John Verdi was a firm believer in quality training and he wanted to send as many of us to the USAF Fighter Weapons School at Nellis AFB as he could. The Marine Corps said, "We don't have any money to send Marine pilots to an Air Force school." Verdi said the hell with the Marine Corps, I'll take care of this in my own way. He promptly contacted a couple of the Fighter Weapons instructors and invited them to visit El Toro on a weekend. As far as the Air Force was concerned, they were just on a cross country training flight when they arrived on a Friday afternoon in two brand-new camouflaged F-4s. We started our 'Fighter Weapons School' immediately with lectures, then flights with a Marine in the back seat of each of those F-4s, while we went up against them in our F-4s. It was a memorable weekend. Those Air Force airplanes even smelled new and those USAF instructors were great guys! We flew all day Saturday and Sunday with them...and it was a very valuable experience, although all totally unofficial. This was a typical example of how Verdi got the job done in spite of any obstacles thrown up in front of him, from their side or ours. There may have been some repercussions from this, but if there were, we never heard them. That was also typical. He managed to insulate us from higher headquarters, which is why there were very few medals handed out to VMFA-122. Verdi's favorite description of selected brass hats was; 'Hydrocephaletic, incompetent communists!'

Verdi was a Reserve Officer, who thought all military men should be reserves and should only be on active duty when there was a war on. He had fought with the French at Dien Bien Phu and when the French withdrew from Vietnam, he got out of the military. He figured the only reason to have regulars was so that there was a cadre to train reservists! The stories about him are almost too numerous to tell in a short narrative like this, but one of the most significant indicators of his effectiveness was that he rose to the rank of full colonel as a reservist, which was a rare occurrence.

Our first experiences with Verdi were pretty rough. For three weeks after he took over the squadron, we hardly saw him. When he wasn't flying cross countries to other Navy, Marine, or Air Force bases, he was behind locked doors. When he finally called his first meeting of all officers, it was to administer a royal chewing-out. He had spent three weeks traveling to other bases, determining what could be accomplished with an all-out effort and he had come to the conclusion that we were sadly lacking in operational readiness. Of course, it wasn't the fault of John Hudson, who had been denied airplanes, spare parts and pilots, but Verdi wanted to make the point that a new day had dawned and that we had better shape up...and damn quick! He terrified us and that was not a bad way to start out...it could only go one way after that...up...and it did.

Our first combat mission in Vietnam was an orientation flight...an area familiarization flight, conducted by VMFA-235, which was flying F-8 Crusaders. Our CO (Verdi) flew wing on a Crusader, flown (I think) by 235's CO. Before they could get to the target, Verdi discovered that his wing tanks would not feed and he would not have enough internal fuel to finish the mission. He was forced to leave the F-8 out there and come home. After he landed, he didn't even go to the fuel pits...he just taxied back to the line and parked it. I was Flight Line Officer and bore the brunt of his displeasure, which was vocal and demonstrative! He just would not accept anything less than perfection and

During 1972, VMFA-115 Phantoms operated from Nam Phong, Thailand. This F-4B is carrying a load of four shot Zuni rocket pods on the inboard wing stations. (Santucci)

CHAOS was a Vietnam combat veteran assigned to VMFA-115. VMFA-115 was based at Atsugi, Japan, during March of 1971.

he did not hesitate to express his displeasure when pilots or equipment didn't measure up to his standard.

The missions that gave me the most satisfaction were those close air support missions where you knew you had saved the lives of some of our Marines. One mission that is particularly memorable was flown against an enemy that we could not see, but knew was there.

During the siege of Khe Sanh, our Marines occupied two hills within a few hundred yards of the base. These two hills were separated by a saddle that couldn't have been more than twenty yards wide. Khe Sanh was virtually surrounded by the North Vietnamese and, while they never managed a major frontal assault, they kept the pressure on with mortar, rocket and sniper fire. The area around Khe Sanh was honeycombed by their trenches and tunnels as they sought to infiltrate American lines. When the Marines on those two hills were surrounded, we laid on an all-out effort to save them. It was too hot an area to try to extract them by helicopter and the best we could do was drop ammunition and supplies via parachute. The North Vietnamese attacks were beaten back by the Marines, but that didn't stop the NVA from making a concerted effort to wipe out the Marines. Marine medics, using their stethoscopes, listened to the enemy tunneling into and under their hill. The implications were pretty obvious. The North Vietnamese were expert tunnel builders. They would either come up with another way to access the hilltops, or they would pack the hills with explosives and blow them away. The only way to discourage this was with massive amounts of close air support. Our bombs fell so close that they caused concussions among our troops, but we sure put an end to the NVA tunneling activities. Our reward was a lot of calls from thankful Marines who had been on that hill with what they considered uncertain futures before we showed up and sealed the tombs on those gooks.

John Verdi called supply people 'Enemies of the American public.' His reasoning went like this; The American public, through taxes approved by Congress, bought and paid for certain items of military hardware. When we couldn't get them through normal supply channels, it was because the supply people were not doing their jobs; hence, they were enemies of the taxpayers, who had paid for the hardware. He was particularly incensed if he discovered that something existed that would, in his judgment, make our jobs easier and that something was not being passed along to us. A case in point was the Snakeye fins for 750 pound bombs. Snakeye fins operate like speed brakes on an airplane, deploying when the bomb is dropped. This retards the time from release until impact, allowing the bomber to drop his bombs at lower altitude, thereby being able to achieve more accuracy and still escape the blast of his own bombs. Snakeyes were commonly used for close air support, where pinpoint accuracy was a must and the most popular sizes were 250 and 500 pounders. Nobody had ever seen a 750 snake...it just seemed too big for close air support, since you couldn't get one of those things too close to your own troops, for fear of hurting them.

Somehow Verdi found out about the 750 pound Snakeyes. Naturally he said, "The damn supply people — enemies of the American public — have got them and they aren't making them available! I want them!" And somehow, he got them. I only flew one mission with the "snaked" 750s. Howard DeCastro, one of the best pilots in our squadron, was my wingman and we had

one hell of a time getting rid of those damn things! We went from FAC to FAC, and each time they heard what we had, they turned us down. A snaked 750 was like a snaked nuke to the troops...you could get it real close to them, but they didn't like it any more than the enemy. The FACs, most of them very experienced, had never heard of these things and we had a tough time convincing them that we really did have 750 snakes. We finally ended up dropping them in the DMZ, where they couldn't hurt anybody except the enemy. That was the last we saw of the 750 pound Snakeyes.

There were not more than a half dozen of us who spent their entire tour in the squadron. VMFA-122 was unusual for the Vietnam War in that we came in country as a unit and we would have left as a unit, had we remained intact through the entire thirteen month tour. The Marine Corps figured this out about two thirds of the way through our tour and began the process of transferring people in and out of the squadron, to make sure that an adequate experience base remained in the unit, no matter who came or went. In that way, we were just like all the other Marine or Air Force units fighting the air war. But in many other ways, we were unique. For instance, unlike the Air Force, we were not under positive control on our missions. We were able to take off, contact a FAC or FACs, and hit the targets that were most opportune. Or we were able to do armed reconnaissances, hitting targets of opportunity. We pretty much went wherever we wanted within our area of operations. That kind of flexibility made for very effective air support and it was very popular with the pilots.

On the other hand, the Air Force F-4 squadron on base was hamstrung by rules and regulations. We got to know their pilots well because we often spent some memorable hours together at the Officer's Clubs. We allowed them to come over and fly with us, in our airplanes. We could get away with that. They couldn't. That was not the only interaction we had with them. They had a marvelous supply system, but there was one item they never seemed to get enough of, which we had in abundance. One of the great features of the F-4 is it's tailhook, which allows field arrested landings. Great when you have battle damage that might mean no brakes or no flaps. The Air Force was just not used to having airplanes with tailhooks and they never seemed to be able to get tailhook points. We traded those points for everything

A pair of VMFA-115 Phantoms prepare for a section takeoff at Yokota, Japan, during October of 1974. Marine squadrons in Japan were ready to return to Vietnam if called upon. (Masumi Wada via Jack Bol via Jim Sullivan)

Joker was the aircraft assigned to the commander of Marine Air Group 15 during August of 1973 and carries the Air Group insignia on the fuselage side. (Shinichi Ohtaki)

VMFA-115 saw its last Vietnam War action covering the evacuation of Saigon in April of 1975, while deployed aboard USS ENTERPRISE in the South China Sea. In the background is the Phantom's replacement, an F-14 Tomcat of VF-1. (U.S. Navy by PH1 James Lumzer)

from spare parts to wall lockers.

You have heard the story about Tiger Island, off the coast of Vietnam, opposite the DMZ. We practiced our loft bombing there and some of us got pretty good at it. I got a chance to use what I had learned on an A-6 escort mission in the DMZ. The A-6 was tasked with laying mines in the Ben Hai river, which runs through the DMZ. Laying mines requires a relatively low and slow profile, which would make the A-6 a sitting duck for the NVA gunners along the north side of the river. I was assigned the job of laying CBUs on the NVA to discourage them from firing at the A-6. The only problem was that the weather was terrible. The ceiling was less than 500 feet, with no more than a couple of miles of visibility. You can't drop CBUs from that low, because they won't arm and break open as they were designed to. I decided to use what I had learned from my loft bombing missions against Tiger Island. I came in from the south, at 200 feet, using Dong Ha as my IP. I spotted the target and, using the experience I had gained at Tiger Island, pulled up into the clouds, pickled off the CBUs, and did a wingover in the clouds. I came out the bottom in time to see all those bomblets exploding all over the NVA positions. It may have been my proudest moment in Vietnam. I had called the A-6 in to coincide with by drop and he was able to skate through the target area without getting shot at. (He later wrote me, saying that he didn't even think he could have found the river without a full system A-6, with all it's sophisticated navigation equipment. He realized that I had done the whole thing VFR.)

Howard DeCastro, who was a fantastic air-to-air pilot and later was named Marine Aviator of the year, was involved in one of the more bizarre incidents of our tour. One day, sitting alert on the Hot Pad, Howard calmly walked out to a C-47 which was sitting at the end of the runway, awaiting takeoff clearance. He banged on the side of the fuselage until they opened the door, then climbed aboard. The Gooney took off and we had no idea where it was going, or where Howard landed. We would have been more amazed, but at the time the book 'Catch 22' was going around the squadron and we all felt that our unit fit the

mold of Yossarian's outfit in the book. Three days later I was the night maintenance duty officer. The phone rang and it was Howard. Somehow he had gotten through on the telephone from Ubon RTAB, Thailand. He was in the Officer's Club and was obviously in his cups.

He said, "Dougal, I'm over here at Ubon. Steal an airplane and come get me!" This was late in our tour and Verdi had been replaced. His replacement would never have consented to this rescue mission and we both knew it, which is why Howard wanted me to steal an airplane. I told him it would be impossible. We didn't even have any missions scheduled and there was no reason for me to take off. But he persisted and I finally agreed to go talk to the XO about retrieving him. The XO gave me all the reasons why I couldn't go, but he never really said no and sometimes in the Marine Corps, silence is permission. I decided that that's what it was in this case. I went back to the squadron, got an airplane, and loaded all of Howard's flight gear into the back seat, tied it down and took off. The controller, of course, asked me where I was going, but I faked a radio failure and headed for Ubon.

Howard had climbed on that C-47 in his smelly, sweaty flight suit and nothing else, including money. But he is a great guy...a real personality...and he proved it to me that night. When I walked into the Officers Club at Ubon, there was Howard at the bar, in a suit, buying people drinks. He had just finished telling all the Air Force types that his buddy was going to steal an airplane and come over from Danang to pick him up. Well, those kinds of things just can't happen in the Air Force and no one believed him. At that moment, I walked in the bar with his flight gear under my arm, grabbed him, and said, "Howard, let's get the hell out of here before they find out the airplane is gone!"

Those Air Force guys couldn't believe it! Howard changed into his flight suit right there in the bar, gave the borrowed clothes back to the generous Air Force type who still couldn't believe what was happening. Howard was so drunk he could hardly walk, but we managed to get him out to the airplane. The line crew was fueling us and I was real anxious to get on my way, when I spotted the duty officer heading our way in is car. The Air Force had a habit of treating you like a guest...almost like they do here in the States and the duty officer was going to make sure

An F-4B of VMFA-115 on the ramp at Misawa Air Base, Japan, on 17 August 1974. This F-4B (BuNo 153036) was assigned to VMFA-115's Commanding Officer and was normally based at MCAS Iwakuni, Japan. (Norman E. Taylor)

This Phantom was a recent arrival with VMFA-323 and had not yet been painted with the squadron's markings. It is loaded with M-117 750 pound bombs. VFMA-323 was part of MAG-13 at Chu Lai during December of 1967. (USMC)

COL D.D. Petty, Jr., commanding officer of Marine Air Group 13 (MAG-13) at Chu Lai, makes the 1,000th arrested landing at the base on 17 November 1967, in an F-4B from VMFA-323. (USMC)

that we were treated well. I knew that if he saw Howard in the condition he was in that he would never let us take off, so I shooed Howard off into the grass, told him to lie down and not say a word. After I had assured the duty officer that we had been treated well and would soon be out of his hair, he drove off. I got Howard strapped in, put his oxygen mask on and he was out like a light.

We got off about 0330 and headed for Danang, with Howard strictly a passenger. I was about 75 miles out of Danang and thinking that I was going to sneak back in there and actually pull off this improbable rescue, when suddenly my radar in the front cockpit came to life. I knew that that meant that Howard had turned it on from the back seat. Howard was no back-seater, but he knew how to turn on the radar from the casual experience we all got in the RIOs seat. The next thing I heard on the intercom was, "Let's run some intercepts!" I said, "Howard, go back to sleep!" He wouldn't relent though and was already playing with the radar. I kept telling him to just relax and we would be home shortly, but he had become the intransigent drunk and threatened to talk on the radio if I didn't run some practice intercepts. Well, I sure didn't want him talking on the radio in his condition, so I gave in and ran some intercepts on some local traffic, which I am sure, never knew we were there. I finally managed to get him home from his three days of "MIA".

Another example of some the creative operational decisions that were made happened on a mission I flew into Laos. There was a Special Forces camp that was in real danger of being overrun and we were trying to drive the enemy off with close air support. The weather all over Northern South Vietnam and Laos was terrible and it was tough getting airplanes to the targets. We got there, expended all our ordnance, but the North Vietnamese were still attacking. I dropped my empty rocket pods on them, then made too many dry runs, trying to get them to break off the attack. I was at bingo fuel minus when I finally pulled off. The controllers told me that I was about the twentieth guy in line for Danang and that all of us had low fuel emergen-

This F-4B of VMFA-323 at Chu Lai during 1967, carries Triple Ejector Racks (TERs) on the inboard wing stations, a Multiple Ejector Rack (MER) on the centerline station and two napalm bombs on the starboard wing. (Manny Simpson)

cies. I knew I would never get into Danang before I ran out of gas, so I headed for Ubon. I just barely made it, only because I cleaned everything off the airplane, including MERs, TERs and drop tanks.

My biggest concern, after landing, was how I was going to explain to Verdi why I had to jettison those tanks, which were in real short supply in the squadron. I just knew he was going to have my butt! Once again Air Force generosity saved the day. I begged the line guys to load a pair of wing tanks on when they refueled me and they agreed. Then I thought, "Well, as long as I'm going back that way anyway, why not load up with bombs and do some good?" They obliged my request for a MER and a pair of TERs and loaded me with bombs. I contacted a FAC on the way back and got rid of that Air Force ordinance. There was a lot of head-scratching back at the squadron when I landed with those camouflaged wing tanks and that airplane carried those tanks for several weeks after that mission.

Marine pilots have great sympathy for the grunts. Most of us would not like to go to war with the grunts, so we took every opportunity to entertain them when we weren't saving them with close air support. I had a good friend who was a battalion ground FAC and whenever I finished a mission in his area, I would make it a point to make a low pass over his position. Now, his CO had no use whatsoever for aviators and would have screamed bloody murder if we put on an impromptu air show. But the troops liked airshows, my buddy liked air shows, and most of the other officers liked airshows, so we established a radio code word, and when he was around, I would make that low pass. If his CO was also around, he would pop a red smoke grenade and I would head back to Danang. If the coast was clear, he would pop yellow smoke and I would make several low passes and some aileron rolls. We must have put on twenty or more of these airshows before I blew the barber shop tent down, along with most of the clotheslines one day. That finished the popularity of the airshows with the troops. Our FACs (Marine pilots did duty as ground FAC with the infantry units) were out there and they appreciated the fact that we knew they were there and were looking out for them. These unscheduled airshows were a good way to pump them up and entertain the troops. The Phantom was big, fast and noisy. A great airplane for that kind of airshow.

In most cases arrested landings were not necessary and Phantoms landing at Chu Lai used drag chutes and brakes. MOREST arrested landings became necessary when the 8,000 foot aluminum mat runway was wet or there were unfavorable winds. (USMC)

Jack McEncroe poses in front of his Phantom before a mission during July of 1968. The Phantom is loaded with bombs and Zuni rocket tubes on the wing stations and napalm tanks on the centerline station. (Jack McEncroe)

These seven F-4Bs of VMFA-323 staged through NAHA Air Base on Okinawa while enroute to Vietnam during 1966. (U.S. Navy via Chuck Mayer)

An F-4B of VMFA-323 makes an arrested landing at Chu Lai on 14 October 1967. The undercoat of asphalt used to widen the runway at Chu Lai is evident. Maintenance of the runway at Chu Lai was an ongoing project that took all the expertise of the Marine construction crews. (USMC)

This F-4B Phantom was written off because of a crash landing during August of 1968. The F-4 was cannibalized for parts to keep the rest of the squadron's Phantoms operational. (Jack McEncroe)

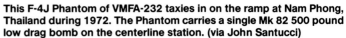

This F-4J Phantom of VMFA-232 taxies in on the ramp at Nam Phong, Thailand during 1972. The Phantom carries a single Mk 82 500 pound low drag bomb on the centerline station. (via John Santucci)

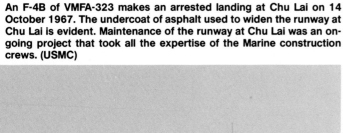

(Above) An F-4J of VMFA-334 taxies in at Danang after a 1968 mission. VMFA-334 was the first Marine fighter squadron to leave Vietnam under President Nixon's troop withdrawal plan. The Falcons moved to MCAS Iwakuni, Japan. (USMC)

(Below) VMFA-232's unit markings evolved from a fairly plain tail with the unit insignia in a Red bordered White box, to this Red tailed Phantom with a much larger Red Devil insignia.

(Above) A VMFA-232 Phantom at Nam Phong, Thailand. The base had been begun in 1967, suspended in 1968, and quickly finished in 1972 by Seabees. VMF-115 and 232 moved there from Danang that year. (via John Santucci)

(Below) VMFA-232 had flown the LTV F-8 Crusader in combat in Vietnam. When they transitioned to the F-4J, they remained at MCAS Iwakuni until the 1972 Easter Invasion of South Vietnam forced their transfer back into the war zone. (Shinichi Ohtaki)

47

Combat Epilog

The last shots fired in anger by Marine Phantoms were fired at the end of American involvement in the Vietnam War. The Phantom, however, continued to serve as a front line combat fighter with the Marines long after Vietnam. During the immediate post-war years the role of the Phantom was perhaps even more important than it had been during the fighting.

The unilateral pullout from Southeast Asia had sent all the wrong signals to America's enemies. There seemed to be a decline in the political will to be the defender of liberty in the world, a perception that would remain until the advent of the Reagan years. Under those circumstances, it was vital that America's military was capable of projecting the force necessary to carry out American foreign policy.

The Marines have always been in the forefront of that projection of power. They are often the first military forces to land on foreign shores and their close air support was provided by their own aircraft. As we left Vietnam, the most powerful aircraft in the Marine inventory was the Phantom and until it was replaced by the F/A-18 Hornet during the late 1980s, the Phantom was the aircraft relied upon to provide close air support, combat air patrol, and reconnaissance for

F-4J (BuNo 155737ah) of VMFA-334 on the ramp at Ubon RTAFB, Thailand, during a 1968 fuel stop. Marine Phantoms normally flew with fuel tanks on the outboard wing stations. (Al Piccirillo via Norm Taylor)

the Marines. So, while the Marine F-4s were not called upon to engage an enemy from the end of Vietnam until their retirement from active service, they still performed a vital mission.

(Above) An F-4J of VMFA-334 on final approach for landing at NAS Atsugi, Japan, after a functional check flight on 27 May 1970. The lightning bolt on the fin and bird on the fuselage are in Red. (Shinichi Ohtaki)

(Below) An F-4J of VMFA-232 over Yokota Air Base, Japan, during 1973. The squadron returned to Japan after the Vietnamese cease-fire and the cut-off of combat support funds by Congress. (Norm Taylor)

With its drag chute deployed, a plain tailed F-4J Phantom (BuNo 153796) of VMFA-232 rolls out on the runway at MCAS Iwakuni, Japan. (Norm Taylor)

(Above) There were many F-4 squadrons which did not see combat in Vietnam and the Marines continued to fly the F-4 long after the Vietnam War. One of those squadrons was VMFA-513 Flying Nightmares, based at MCAS Cherry Point during April of 1970. (USMC via Jack Hunt)

(Below) A Red and White Satan's head is painted on the splitter plate of this F-4J (BuNo 155801ai) of VMFA-232 at Misawa AB, Japan, on 19 July 1974. The names on the canopy rail are in White against a Red background. (Norman E. Taylor)

During 1966, VMFA-312 carried Black and White checkerboard squadron markings across the top of the fin and rudder with a thin Red border across the bottom and a thin Yellow border across the top of the checkerboard. (Norman E. Taylor)

An F-4B of VMFA-312, 2nd Marine Air Wing, in the markings carried by the squadron during 1972. The Checkerboard on the tail is now carried in a chevron style with a Red outline below and a Yellow outline above the chevron. (Norman E. Taylor)

(Above) By the 1980s the camouflage carried on the Phantom had changed to overall flat Gull Gray. The earlier White undersurfaces were meant to reflect the energy of nuclear explosions. As the nuclear option became remote and dogfights with enemy fighters became a more realistic threat, the camouflage was changed to suit the threat. The squadron markings were in Black and shades of Gray. (Norm Taylor Collection)

(Below) The latest camouflage carried by Phantoms of VMFA-312 is a low-visibility Gray scheme intended primarily for air-to-air combat. All national, service and unit markings are in various shades of Gray with no White or Black carried on the aircraft. (Campbell)

This F-4B (BuNo 151437) of VMFA-251 Thunderbolts is parked on the ramp of MCAS Beaufort, S.C., during the Fall of 1968. MCAS Beaufort was the site where the movie "The Great Santini" was filmed. (USMC via Jack Hunt)

An F-4S Phantom of VMFA-251 on the ramp at MCAS Beaufort during 1980. The F-4S was a follow-on improvement of the F-4J which featured maneuvering slats on the wing leading edge, as well as more sophisticated avionics. (Fred Harl via Norm Taylor)

An F-4J of VMFA-333 Shamrocks at MCAS Beaufort in December of 1969. The unit markings consisted of three Green shamrocks on a White field bordered by Green stripes. (USMC via Jack Hunt)

A VMFA-333 Phantom on the flight line at Beaufort during May of 1985. "Bear" Lasseter and "Little John" Cummings became the first Marine crew to score an aerial victory in Vietnam when they shot down a MiG-21 on 11 September 1972. They were in turn shot down by a SAM on the same mission. They were flying off USS AMERICA (CV-66) at the time. (Fred Harl via Norm Taylor)

When VMFA-235 turned in their F-8 Crusaders for F-4J Phantoms, CAPT Manny Simpson designed four paint schemes, two of which were actually applied to squadron Phantoms. This Phantom was painted in the scheme which was not selected (the winning design featured a star-spangled Red nose). (Simpson)

Older Phantoms began going into storage at MASDC, Davis Monthan AFB, Arizona, during the early 1970s. This F-4B (BuNo 149435) of VMFA-531 is being prepared for storage during June of 1973. (G. Geer via Norm Taylor)

A section of F-4N Phantoms of VMFA-531 patrol over the Indian Ocean during April of 1980. The Phantoms are armed with AIM-9 Sidewinder air-to-air missiles on the inboard wing stations. (U.S. Navy)

(Above) Many F-4Bs were upgraded to F-4N standards with improved avionics, ECM gear and strengthened wings. This Phantom (BuNo 161007) is an F-4N assigned to VMFA-531 during the 1980s. (Norm Taylor)

(Below) Marines began flying from carriers on a regular basis during 1971, after a nearly ten year hiatus. The practice has continued to this day. VMFA-531 flew its F-4Ns from USS CORAL SEA (CV-43) while deployed to the Indian Ocean during 1980. (U.S. Navy)

A pair of F-4Ns (BuNo 150640 in the foreground) of VMFA-323 on the ramp at Tyndall AFB, Florida, during a cross country flight on 21 November 1979. (USAF via Norm Taylor)

VMFA-323 changed squadron markings during 1972 to include a White skull for their rattlesnake to coil around. These Phantoms were on a refueling stop at Kelly AFB, Texas, on 13 October 1972. (Norman E. Taylor)

The ultimate Aggressor aircraft; a pair of USAF flown MiG-21 Fishbeds escort a Phantom of VMFA-323 over the Nevada desert. The USAF received a number of ex-Algerian Air Force MiG-21s from the Israelis after the Six Day War of 1967. The MiGs were operated from a secret base in Nevada in the Aggressor role. (Not an official photo)

A VMFAT-101 F-4B taxies in to the flight line at Tyndall AFB, Florida, on 22 September 1972 for the William Tell weapons meet. The meet is held at Tyndall on even numbered years during late September and early October. (Norman E. Taylor)

(Above) An F-4J (BuNo 153888) of VMFA-451 chocked on the ramp at Tyndall AFB, Florida, on 21 November 1979. At this time, the Warlords were based at MCAS Beaufort, S.C. (Norm Taylor Collection)

(Below) This VMFAT-101 Phantom carries what every fighter pilot would consider the most appropriate tail code for his airplane, Sierra Hotel. (Shinichi Ohtaki)

(Above) This F-4S (BuNo 157301) carries the Warlords squadron markings in the subdued air-to-air Gray camouflage at MCAS Beaufort, on 16 September 1986. (Norm Taylor)

(Below) VMFA-314 adopted the all Black tail with White tail codes that were favored by many Navy Phantom squadrons for their F-4Ns during 1981. The Knight's helmet on the fuselage is in Black and White. (Norm Taylor)

This F-4N (BuNo 152208) was one of 228 F-4Bs modified under the Navy's Service Life Extension Program (SLEP) which updated the systems and improved the airframes of F-4Bs giving them a new lease on life. (Norm Taylor)

VMFA-122 eventually transitioned to the F-4S. Three of the Phantoms carry the transitional overall Flat Gull Gray camouflage scheme, which allowed full size/color national and service markings, while the last three aircraft have been painted in the latest subdued Navy/Marine Phantom camouflage scheme. (Norm Taylor)

This F-4S (BuNo 153800) of VMFA-122 was modified from the first F-4J of the block nineteen series aircraft and carries the overall Gloss Dark Gull Gray camouflage scheme in use during 1981. (Fred Harl via Norman E. Taylor)

This F-4J (BuNo 153798) of VMFA-212 Lancers was assigned to the Commanding Officer of MAG 21, based at MCAS Kaneohe, Hawaii, on 16 January 1975. The Phantom carries a Pineapple on the splinter plate. (Dr. J.G. Handelman)

This F-4J (BuNo 155823) was one of the J models converted to F-4S standards and assigned to VMFA-115. This Phantom carries the squadron's special Bicentennial markings.

This VMFA-115 F-4S (BuNo 155825, from a block 20 F-4J) Phantom carried an unusual camouflage scheme of overall Gloss Dark Gull Gray with White unit and service markings during November of 1979 at NAS Miramar, California. VMFA-115 was part of the 1st Marine Air Wing. (U.S. Navy)

An F-4B of VMFA-321 at NAS Andrews, Washington, D.C. on 9 May 1975. Recognizing the necessity to pass on lessons learned in Vietnam, the Marines established a program aimed at teaching direct support. Marine Aviation Weapons and Tactics Squadron One (MAWTS-1) at MCAS Yuma, Arizona, is assigned the mission and during 1978, all Marine squadrons sent representatives to MAWTS. (C. Eddy via Norman E. Taylor)

An F-4S (BuNo 153884) of VMFA-321 at NAS Andrews on 4 September 1987. This Phantom carries air-to-air missile simulator pods on the inboard wing stations and the latest air-to-air camouflage. (G. Cockle via Norm Taylor)

An F-4B Phantom (BuNo 150429) of VMFAT-201 on the ramp at MCAS Cherry Point, North Carolina during May of 1969. VMFAT squadrons are tactical training units that teach F-4 combat operations to new Phantom crews. (USMC via Jim Sullivan)

A flight of four F-4s of MAG-11 (VMFA-531, 323, 314 and VMCJ-3) fly over the California desert during group training on 17 May 1969. (via Roy Stafford)

This flight of Fleet Marine Force Pacific (FMFPAC) aircraft from MAG-11 includes F-4Bs of VFMA-314, 323, and 531, along with an RF-4B and EA-6A of VMCJ-3. Both types were in the twilight of their careers with the F/A-18 replacing the F-4. (via Roy Stafford)

The MiG-killing success of VF-96 and VF-161 prompted many Phantom squadrons to paint the tails of their Phantoms overall Black, including reconnaissance squadrons! This Black tailed VMCJ-1 RF-4B is on final approach for landing at MCAS Iwakuni, Japan, during 1972. (Norm Taylor Collection)

This RF-4B of VMCJ-2 Playboys has pulled enough Gs to create wingtip vortice contrails in the humid air over MCAS Cherry Point, N.C. (via Roy Stafford)

An RF-4B of the newly formed composite photo squadron, VMFP-3, catches a wire aboard USS KITTY HAWK (CV-63). The squadron was aboard for its annual carrier qualifications during 1976. (McDonnell Douglas by Harry Gann via Roy Stafford)

This RF-4B (BuNo 153099) was one of six Block 25 aircraft built and was assigned to VMCJ-2 early in its service life. The Marines were the only service to operate the photo reconnaissance RF-4B. (via Roy Stafford)

An RF-4B of VMCJ-2 is positioned on the catapult during carrier qualifications. RF-4Bs are equipped with Martin-Baker Mk H-7 ejection seats, capable of providing safe ejection throughout the Phantom's flight envelope. (via Roy Stafford.)

Four RF-4Bs of VMCJ-3 over the mountains of Southern California. A total of forty-six RF-4Bs were built for the Marine Corps. The Phantom in the foreground (BuNo 151983) is an RF-4B-23-MC. (via Roy Stafford)

This RF-4B-21-MC (BuNo 151978) of VMFP-3 carries the squadron's distinctive Green and Gold tail markings. Marine photo squadrons VMCJ-1, 2, and 3 were consolidated into one squadron, VMFP-3, during 1975 and based at MCAS El Toro. (Shinichi Ohtaki)

VMFP-3's Green and Gold markings eventually gave way to tactical Gray during the mid-1980s. This RF-4B, which survived the Vietnam War, was updated under project SURE (Sensor Update and Refurbishment Effort) during the late 70s.

This RF-4B-24-MC of VMFP-3 stopped at Shaw AFB, S.C. during a cross country flight, on 22 July 1986. A total of twenty-nine RF-4Bs were modified under SURE by NARF North Island. They received AN/ASN-92 Carrier Alignment Inertial Navigation System (CAINS), AN/ASW-25B Data Link System, AN/APD-10 Side Looking Radar, and AN/AAD-5 Infrared Reconnaissance Set. (Norman E. Taylor)

The well known Phantom Spook character is carried on the tail of this VMFP-3 Phantom at El Toro during 1984. The Black Spook is about as individualistic as squadron markings are allowed to get with the tactical Gray camouflage now in use. (Norm Taylor)

A sad end for an historic airplane. The number three production F4H-1 Phantom sits weathering outside the Marine Corps Museum at Quantico, Virginia. This was the first Phantom flown by a Marine, LTCOL R.J. Barbour, who logged his first F-4 hour on 6 October 1959. (via Roy Stafford)

A pair of VMFP-3 Phantoms line up for the catapult aboard USS KITTY HAWK (CV-63) during carrier qualifications. With the retirement of the RF-8 Crusader, responsibility for some fleet reconnaissance missions fell to the RF-4s of the Marine Corps. (McDonnell Douglas)

Vietnam Studies Group
From Squadron/Signal

6002

6042

6037

6046

6351

6352

squadron/signal publication

blur

The Great Escape...

MCA Music Limited

Exclusive Distributors:

Music Sales Limited

8/9 Frith Street, London W1V 5TZ, England.

Music Sales Pty Limited

120 Rothschild Avenue, Rosebery, NSW 2018, Australia.

Order No. AM934770

ISBN 0-7119-5462-3

Original LP cover design by Stylo Rouge.

Book design by Michael Bell Design.

Music arranged by Roger Day.

Music processed by Paul Ewers Music Design.

Front cover photograph courtesy of The Image Bank.

Back cover photograph courtesy of Nels Israelson.

Printed in the United Kingdom By
J.B. Offset Printers (Marks Tey) Limited, Marks Tey, Essex

The Great Escape

Stereotypes

THE SUBURBS THEY ARE DREAMING
THEY ARE A TWINKLE IN HER EYE
SHE'S BEEN FEELING FRISKY
SINCE HER HUSBAND SAID GOODBYE
SHE WEARS A LOW CUT T-SHIRT RUNS A LITTLE B&B
SHE MOST ACCOMMODATING WHEN SHE'S IN HER LINGERIE

WIFE SWAPPING IS THE FUTURE
YOU KNOW THAT IT WOULD SUIT YOU

YES, THEY'RE STEREOTYPES
THERE MUST BE MORE TO LIFE
ALL YOUR LIFE YOU ARE DREAMING
FROM TIME TO TIME YOU KNOW
YOU SHOULD BE GOING ON ANOTHER BENDER

THE SUBURBS THEY ARE SLEEPING
BUT HE'S DRESSING UP TONIGHT
SHE LIKES A MAN IN UNIFORM HE LOVES TO WEAR IT TIGHT
THEY ARE ON THE LOVERS SOFA THEY ARE ON THE PATIO
AND WHEN THE FUN IS OVER WATCH THEMSELVES ON VIDEO

THE NEIGHBOURS MAY BE STARING
BUT THEY ARE JUST PAST CARING

Best Days

BOW BELLS SAY GOODBYE TO THE LAST TRAIN
OVER THE RIVER THEY ALL GO AGAIN
OUT INTO LEAFY NOWHERE HOPE SOMEONE
WAITING OUT THERE FOR THEM
CABBIE HAS HIS MIND ON A FARE TO THE SUN
HE WORKS NIGHT BUT IT'S NOT MUCH FUN
PICKS UP THE LONDON YOYO'S, ALL ON THEIR OWN DOWN SOHO
PLEASE TAKE ME HOME

OTHER PEOPLE WOULDN'T WANT TO HEAR YOU
IF YOU SAID THAT THESE ARE THE BEST DAYS OF THEIR LIVES
OTHER PEOPLE WOULD TURN AROUND AND LAUGH AT YOU
IF YOU SAID THAT THESE WERE THE BEST DAYS OF OUR LIVES

TRELLICK TOWERS BEEN CALLING
I KNOW SHE'LL LEAVE ME IN THE MORNING

IN HOTEL CELLS LISTENING TO DIAL TONES
REMOTE CONTROLS AND CABLE MOANS
IN HIS DRINK HE'S BEEN TALKING
GETS DISCONNECTED SLEEPWALKING BACK HOME

Country House

(SO THE STORY BEGINS)
CITY DWELLER, SUCCESSFUL FELLA
THOUGHT TO HIMSELF
OOPS I'VE GOT ALOT OF MONEY
I'M CAUGHT IN A RAT RACE TERMINALLY
I'M A PROFESSIONAL CYNIC
BUT MY HEARTS NOT IN IT
I'M PAYING THE PRICE OF LIVING LIFE AT THE LEGAL LIMIT
CAUGHT UP IN THE CENTURIES ANXIETY
IT PREYS ON HIM, HE'S GETTING THIN

NOW HE LIVES IN A HOUSE, A VERY BIG HOUSE IN THE COUNTRY
WATCHING AFTERNOON REPEATS
AND THE FOOD HE EATS IN THE COUNTRY
HE TAKES ALL MANNER OF PILLS
AND PILES UP ANALYST BILLS IN THE COUNTRY
IT'S LIKE AN ANIMAL FARM,
LOTS OF RURAL CHARM IN THE COUNTRY

NOW HE'S GOT MORNING GLORY, LIFE'S A DIFFERENT STORY
EVERYTHING GOING JACKANORY
IN TOUCH WITH HIS OWN MORALITY
HE'S READING BALZAC, KNOCKING BACK PROZAC,
IT'S A HELPING HAND
THAT MAKES YOU FEEL WONDERFULLY BLAND
OH, IT'S THE CENTURIES REMEDY FOR THE FAINT AT HEART
A NEW START

HE LIVES IN A HOUSE, A VERY BIG HOUSE IN THE COUNTRY
HE'S GOT A FOG IN HIS CHEST
SO HE NEEDS ALOT OF REST IN THE COUNTRY
HE DOESN'T DRINK SMOKE LAUGH
HE TAKES HERBAL BATHS IN THE COUNTRY
OH, IT'S LIKE AN ANIMAL FARM
BUT YOU'LL COME TO NO HARM IN THE COUNTRY
BLOW BLOW ME OUT I AM SO SAD I DON'T KNOW WHY

Charmless Man

I MET HIM IN A CROWDED ROOM
WHERE PEOPLE GO TO DRINK AWAY THEIR GLOOM
HE SAT ME DOWN AND SO BEGAN, THE STORY OF A CHARMLESS MAN
EDUCATED THE EXPENSIVE WAY, HE KNOWS HIS CLARET FROM A BEAUJOLAIS
I THINK HE'D LIKE TO OF BEEN RONNIE KRAY
BUT THEN NATURE DIDN'T MAKE HIM THAT WAY

HE THINKS HE'S EDUCATED, AIRS THOSE FAMILY SHARES
WILL PROTECT HIM THAT WE WILL RESPECT HIM
HE MOVES IN CIRCLES OF FRIENDS
WHO JUST PRETEND THAT THEY LIKE HIM
HE DOES THE SAME TO THEM, AND WHEN YOU PUT IT ALL TOGETHER
THERE'S THE MODEL OF A CHARMLESS MAN

HE KNOWS THE SWINGERS AND THEIR CAVALRY
SAYS HE CAN GET IN ANYWHERE FOR FREE
I BEGAN TO GO A LITTLE CROSS EYED
AND FROM THIS CHARMLESS MAN I JUST HAD TO HIDE

HE TALKS AT SPEED HE GETS NOSE BLEEDS
HE DOESN'T SEE HIS DAYS
ARE TUMBLING DOWN UPON HIM
AND YET HE TRIES SO HARD TO PLEASE
HE'S JUST SO KEEN FOR YOU TO LISTEN
BUT NO ONE IS LISTENING
AND WHEN YOU PUT IT ALL TOGETHER
THERE'S THE MODEL OF A CHARMLESS MAN

The Universal

THIS IS THE NEXT CENTURY
THE UNIVERSAL IS FREE
YOU CAN FIND IT ANYWHERE
YES, THE FUTURE HAS BEEN SOLD
EVERY NIGHT WE ARE GONE
AND THE KARAOKE SONGS
WE LIKE TO SING ALONG
ALTHOUGH THE WORDS ARE WRONG

IT REALLY, REALLY, REALLY COULD HAPPEN
WHEN THE DAYS SEEM TO FALL STRAIGHT THROUGH YOU
JUST LET THEM GO

NO ONE HERE IS ALONE
SATELLITES IN EVERY HOME
THE UNIVERSAL IS HERE
HERE FOR EVERYONE
EVERY PAPER THAT YOU READ
SAYS TOMORROW IS YOUR LUCKY DAY
WELL, HERE'S YOUR LUCKY DAY

Fade Away

THEY STUMBLED INTO THEIR LIVES
IN A VAGUE WAY BECAME MAN AND WIFE
ONE GOT THE OTHER THEY DESERVED ONE ANOTHER
THEY SETTLED IN A BRAND NEW TOWN
WITH PEOPLE FROM THE SAME BACKGROUND
THEY KEPT THEMSELVES BUSY
LONGS HOURS LEFT THEM DIZZY
NOW WHEN HE'S IN SHE'S OUT

ALL YOU EVER DO IS FADE AWAY
THEY ARE NOT MAKING PLANS
BECAUSE NOW THEY UNDERSTAND
ALL YOU EVER DO IS FADE AWAY

HE NOTICED HE HAD VISIBLE LINES
SHE WORRIED ABOUT HER BEHIND
THEIR BIRTH HAD BEEN THE DEATH OF THEM
IT DIDN'T REALLY BOTHER THEM
NOW WHEN SHE'S IN, HE'S OUT

TOPMAN

THIS IS A PUBLIC WARNING
BE CAREFUL WHEN YOU ARE OUT
WE ARE HAVING FREAKY WEATHER
THERE'S ALOT OF IT ABOUT
THE TERRACES ARE SWINGING
HE'S A MONKEY ON THE ROOF
YOU'VE SEEN HIM ON THE TELLY
SO LET ME INTRODUCE YOUR HOST TONIGHT

T.O.P.M.A.N.
HE'S NAUGHTY BY NATURE
ON DOUBLES AND CHASERS
HE'S A LITTLE BOY RACER
SHOOTING GUNS ON THE HIGH STREET OF LOVE

IN A CROWD IT'S HARD TO SPOT HIM, BUT ANONYMITY CAN COST
HE'S NEVER CHEAP N' CHEERFUL, HE'S HUGO AND HE'S BOSS
HE'S RIDING THROUGH THE DESERT ON A CAMEL LIGHT
AND ON A MAGIC CARPET, HE'LL FLY AWAY TONIGHT
OPEN SESAME

T.O.P.M.A.N.
SEES HER IN DOUBLE
THEN PUKES ON THE PAVEMENT
LIKES HER ALL CLEAN AND SHAVEN
SHOOTING GUNS ON THE HIGH STREET OF LOVE

Mr. Robinson's Quango

MR. ROBINSON AND HIS QUANGO
DIRTY DEALER, EXPENSIVE CAR
RUNS THE BUSES AND THE EVENING STAR
HE GOT A HAIR PIECE AND HE GOT HERPES
HIS PRIVATE LIFE IS VERY DISCREET
A NICER MAN YOU'LL NEVER GOING TO MEET

A SELF PROFESSED SAVIOUR OF THE DIM RIGHT WING
HE'S GOT RESPITORY PROBLEMS AND A MASONS RING

MR. ROBINSON AND HIS QUANGO
DRINKS WITH THE GENERAL AND THE COUNTY WIVES
YES THE FAMILY BUSINESS IS DOING ALL RIGHT
THEY ARE DOING TANGO'S DOWN IN THE QUANGO'S
HE MAKES THEM TICK AND HE MAKES THEM TOCK
AND IF HE DOESN'T LIKE YOU HE'LL PUT YOU IN THE DOCK

HE JUST SITS IN HIS LEATHER CHAIR AND TWIDDLES HIS THUMBS
GETS HIS SECRETARY IN AND PINCHES HER BUM

HE RAN INTO THE TOILET IN THE TOWN HALL
GOT A BIRO OUT AND WROTE ON THE WALL
I'M WEARING FRENCH KNICKERS ON UNDER MY SUIT
I'VE GOT STOCKING AND SUSPENDERS ON
I'M FEELING RATHER LOOSE

OH I'M A NAUGHTY BOY
OH I'M A NAUGHTY, NAUGHTY BOY

He Thought Of Cars

MOSCOW'S STILL RED
THE YOUNG MAN'S DEAD
GONE TO HEAVEN INSTEAD
THE EVENING NEWS SAYS HE WAS CONFUSED
THE MOTORWAYS WILL ALL MERGE SOON
THEY'VE COME TO SAVE US
THE SPACE INVADERS ARE HERE

HE THOUGHT OF CARS
AND WHERE, WHERE TO DRIVE THEM
AND WHO TO DRIVE THEM WITH
AND THERE, THERE WAS NO ONE, NO ONE

THERE'S A PANIC AT LONDON HEATHROW
EVERYBODY WANTS TO GO UP INTO THE BLUE
BUT THERE'S A TEN YEAR QUEUE
COLUMBIA IS IN TOP GEAR
IT SHOULDN'T SNOW AT THIS TIME OF YEAR
NOW AMERICAS SHOT GONE
AND DONE THE LOT

HE THOUGHT OF PLANES AND WHERE
WHERE TO FLY TO
AND WHO TO FLY THERE WITH
AND THERE, THERE WAS NO ONE, NO ONE

It Could Be You

CHURCHILL GOT HIS LUCKY NUMBER
BUT TOMORROW THERE'S ANOTHER
COULD BE ME COULD BE YOU
NO SILVER SPOON
STICKY TEETH THEY ROT TOO SOON
YOU'VE GOT TO HAVE THE BEST TUNES
OR THAT'S IT YOU'VE BLOWN IT

ALL WE WANT IS TO BE HAPPY
IN OUR HOMES LIKE HAPPY FAMILIES
BE THE MAN ON THE BEACH WITH
THE WORLD AT HIS FEET
YES, IT COULD BE YOU

THE LIKELY LADS
ARE PICKING UP THE UGLIES
YESTERDAY THEY WERE JUST PUPPIES
BEERY SLURS NOW LIFE'S A BLUR
TELLY ADDICTS
YOU SHOULD SEE THEM AT IT
GETTING IN A PANIC
WILL WE BE THERE
TRAFALGAR SQUARE?

SO DON'T WORRY
IF IT'S NOT YOUR LUCKY NUMBER
BECAUSE TOMORROW THERE IS ANOTHER
COULD BE YOU, COULD BE ME

Ernold Same

ERNOLD SAME AWOKE FROM THE SAME DREAM
IN THE SAME BED AT THE SAME TIME
LOOKED IN THE SAME MIRROR
MADE THE SAME FROWN
AND FELT THE SAME WAY AS HE DID EVERY DAY,
THEN ERNOLD SAME CAUGHT THE SAME TRAIN
AT THE SAME STATION, SAT IN THE SAME SEAT
WITH THE SAME NASTY STAIN
NEXT TO SAME OLD WHAT'S HIS NAME
ON HIS WAY TO THE SAME PLACE TO DO THE SAME THING
AGAIN AND AGAIN ... POOR OLD ERNOLD SAME.
OH ERNOLD SAME,
HIS WORLDS STAYS THE SAME,
TODAY WILL ALWAYS BE TOMORROW,
POOR OLD ERNOLD SAME,
HE 'S GETTING THAT FELLING ONCE AGAIN,
NOTHING WILL CHANGE TOMORROW.

Globe Alone

WHO MADDEST ONE ON THE M1
WHO HASN'T STOPPED SUCKING HIS THUMB
WHO VERY STRAIGHT AND NEVER GRINS
WHO CARES WHAT CAR HE'S DRIVING IN

HE IS BECAUSE HE SAW IT ON A COMMERCIAL BREAK
AND IF HE DOESN'T GET WHAT
HE WANTS THEN HE'LL GET A HEADACHE
BECAUSE HE WANTS IT, NEEDS IT, ALMOST LOVES IT
HE'S HERE ON HIS OWN, ON GLOBE ALONE

WHO JOINED HEALTH CLUB TO GLISTEN
INTO HI FI PRECISION
WHO'S MOBILE PHONE GIVES HIM THE BONE
WHO VERY KEEN ON SHARON STONE

WHO ONLY EATS AT THE NEW BRASSERIE
WHO ONLY EVERY GETS MERRY
WHO WOULDN'T BE SEEN AT BED TIME
WITHOUT PUTTING CALVIN KLEINS ON

Dan Abnormal (The Meanie Leanie)

MEANIE LEANIE COME ON DOWN
COME AND ENTERTAIN THE TOWN
IT'S FRIDAY NIGHT AND WE'RE ALL BORED
TIMES BEEN CALLED THERE IS NO MORE
TIMES BEEN CALLED IT'S SUCH A BORE

DAN ABNORMAL NOT NORMAL AT ALL
IT'S NOT HIS FAULT WE MADE HIM THIS WAY
HE'LL IMITATE YOU TRY TO APE YOU
BUT IT'S NOT HIS FAULT DAN WATCHES TV

THE MEANIE LEANIE STAYS UP LATE
MOPES AROUND GETS IN A STATE
HE'S THE KILLER IN YOUR ARCADE
KILLING GANGSTAS READY MADE
CAUSE THAT IS WHERE THE FUTURES MADE

TELE PORT ME

DAN WENT TO HIS LOCAL BURGER BAR
I WANT McNORMAL AND CHIPS
OR I'LL BLOW YOU TO BITS
GIVE US IT

IT'S THE MISERIES AT HALF PAST THREE
WATCHING VIDEO NASTIES
HE HAS DIRTY DREAMS WHILE HE'S ASLEEP
DAN'S JUST LIKE YOU YOU SEE
HE'S THE MEANIE LEANIE

Entertain Me

THE WEEKEND IS BACK
BUT SO IS HE
HEAD TO THE FLOODLIGHTS
SEE THE FRATERNITY
THEY ARE WAITING
I HEAR THEM UP IN THE NORTH
AND DOWN IN THE SOUTH
ALL THAT IS SPEWING
SPEWING OUT OF HIS MOUTH

ENTERTAIN ME
AT HIS AND HERS DATING
BORED MINDS AGREE
REQUIREMENTS TO BE STATED
REPLIES AWAITED
SHE WANTS A LOOSE FIT
HE WANTS INSTANT WHIP
HE GUESSTIMATES HER ARRIVAL
WILL SHE WANT IT REALLY BADLY

ENTERTAIN ME

A CAR, A HOUSE BOTH IN STREET
THE BOREDOM OF THE SOBER WEEK
THE WEEKEND IS HERE, HIP HIP HOORAY
TO MAKE THE BLUES JUST GO AWAY

ENTERTAIN ME

Yuko and Hiro

THIS IS MY WORK PLACE
AND THESE ARE THE PEOPLE I WORK WITH
YUKO AND HIRO
WE WORK TOGETHER
WE WORK FOR THE COMPANY
THAT WORKS TO THE FUTURE
THEY WILL PROTECT US
WE WORK TOGETHER

I NEVER SEE YOU
WE ARE NEVER TOGETHER
I'LL LOVE YOU FOR EVER

I DRINK IN THE EVENINGS
IT HELPS WITH RELAXING
I CAN'T SLEEP WITHOUT DRINKING
WE DRINK TOGETHER
FROM MONDAY TO SATURDAY
I GO TO MY WORKPLACE
BUT ON SUNDAY WE ARE TOGETHER
YUKO AND HIRO

Stereotypes

Words & Music by Damon Albarn, Graham Coxon, Alex James & David Rowntree

⊕ Coda

Verse 2:
The suburbs they are sleeping
But he's dressing up tonight
She likes a man in uniform he loves to wear it tight
They are on the lovers sofa they are on the patio
And when the fun is over watch themselves on video.

The neighbours may be staring
But they are just past caring.

Country House

Words & Music by Damon Albarn, Graham Coxon, Alex James & David Rowntree

food he eats___ in the coun - try. He takes all

man-ner of pills___ and piles up a - na - lyst's bills___ in the coun - try;

Ooh,___ it's like an A - ni - mal Farm,___ lots of ru - ral charm___ in the coun-

1. - try. Oh,___ he - try._____ Ooh, la la

2.

18

Verse 2:
He's got morning glory,
And life's a different story;
Everything's going 'Jackanory'…
In touch with his own mortality.
He's reading Balzac, knocking back Prozac—
It's a helping hand that makes you feel wonderfully bland;
Oh, it's the century's remedy:
For the faint at heart, a new start.

Chorus 2:
He lives in a house, a very big house in the country.
He's got a fog in his chest,
So he needs a lot of rest in the country.
He doesn't drink, smoke, laugh;
Takes herbal baths in the country.
But you'll come to no harm
On the Animal Farm in the country.

Verse 3: Instrumental

19

Best Days

Words & Music by Damon Albarn, Graham Coxon, Alex James & David Rowntree

Hope some-one's wait - ing out____ there for them.

Cab - - bie has his mind on a fare____ to the sun,____ he works

nights but it's not____ much fun,____ picks up the Lon - don yo - yos

all on their own____ down So - ho, take me home.____

Verse 2:
Trellick Tower's been calling
I know she'll leave me in the morning
In hotel cells listening to dial tones
Remote controls and cable moans
In his drink he's talking
Gets disconnected sleepwalking back home.

Charmless Man

Words & Music by Damon Albarn, Graham Coxon, Alex James & David Rowntree

Verse 2:

He knows the swingers and their cavalry
Says he can get in anywhere for free
I began to go a little cross-eyed
And from this charmless man I just had to hide.

La la la…

He talks at speed, he gets nose-bleeds
He doesn't see his days are tumbling down upon him
Cnd yet he tries so hard to please
He's just so keen for you to listen but no one is listening
And when you put it all together
There's the model of a charmless man.

𝄋

He thinks he's educated, airs those family shares
Will protect him, that you'll respect him
And yet he tries so hard to please
He's so keen for you to listen, but no one's listening
And when you put it all together
There's the model of a charmless man.

Mr. Robinson's Quango

Words & Music by Damon Albarn, Graham Coxon, Alex James & David Rowntree

runs the bus - es and the Eve - ning Star____ He got a hair piece, he got

her - pes. His pri - vate life____ is ve - ry dis - creet, a

He's the self-pro-fessed sa-viour of the dim right wing, he's got res-
nic - er man no you're nev - er gon - na meet.

- p'ra - to - ry prob - lems and a ma - son's ring.____

black French knick-ers un-der my suit,— I got stock-ings and sus-pen-ders on, I'm feel-ing ra-ther loose.—

Oh, I'm a naugh-ty boy,— oh, I'm a naugh-ty, naugh-ty boy.—

Verse 2:
Oh Mister Robinson and his quango
Drinks with generals and county wives
The family business is doing all right.
They're doing tangos down in the quangos
He makes them tick, oh he makes them tock
And if you don't fit he'll put you in the dock.

He just sits in his leather chair and twiddles his thumbs
Gets his secretary in and pinches her bum.

Fade Away

Words & Music by Damon Albarn, Graham Coxon, Alex James & David Rowntree

served one an- oth - er. They

set - tled in a brand new town, with
(Verse 2 see block lyric)

peo - ple from the same back - ground, they

kept them- selves bu - sy, long ho- urs left them diz - zy, now when he's in

37

All you ev-er do is fade a-way,

all you ev-er do is fade a-way.

1.
They're not mak-ing plans 'cause now they un-der-stand, you must

Verse 2:
He noticed he had visible lines
She worried about her behind
Their birth had been the death of them
It didn't really bother them
Now when she's in, he's out.

Top Man

Words & Music by Damon Albarn, Graham Coxon, Alex James & David Rowntree

is a pub-lic warn-ing
(Verse 2 see block lyric)
be care-ful when you're out.

We're hav-ing frea-ky— wea-ther, there's a

lot of it a-bout. On the ter-ra-ces it's swing-ing,

he's a mon-key on the roof. You've

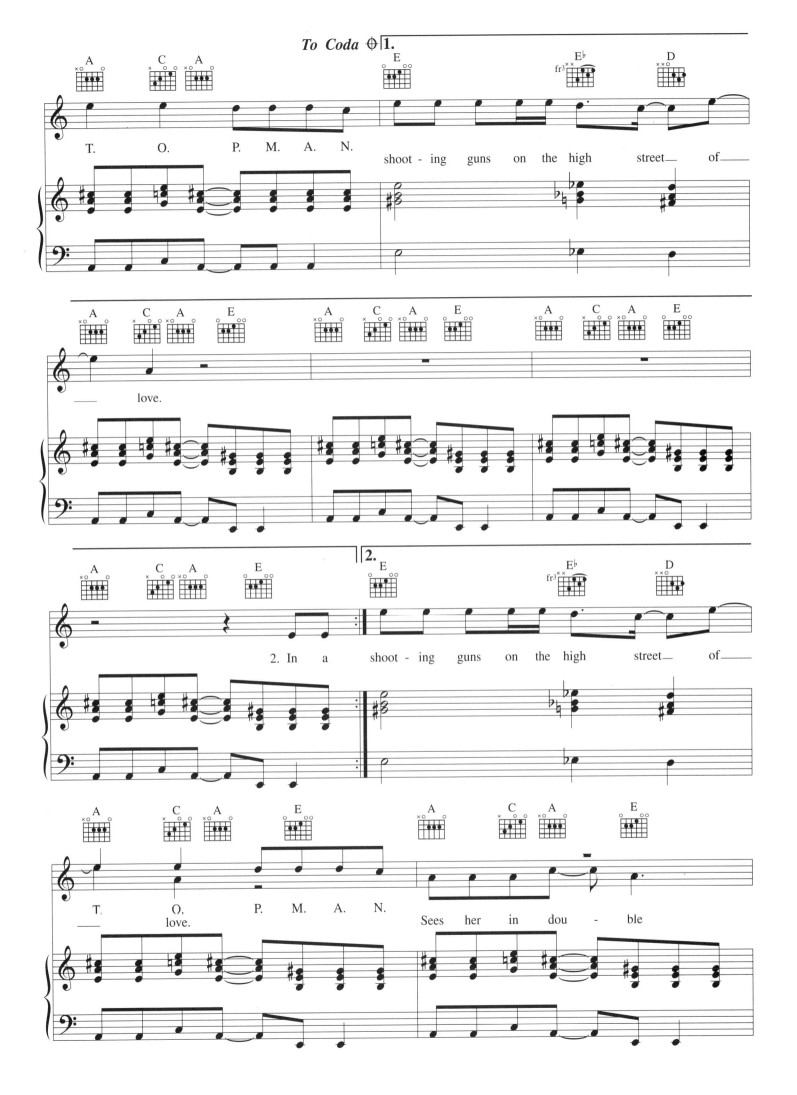

shoot-ing guns on the high street _ of _ love.   Shoot-ing guns on the high street _ of _

Verse 2:
In a crowd it's hard to spot him
Anonymity can cost.
He's never cheap 'n' cheerful
He's Hugo and he's boss.
He's riding through the desert
On a camel light
And on a magic carpet
He'll fly away tonight.
Open Sesame!

The Universal

Words & Music by Damon Albarn, Graham Coxon, Alex James & David Rowntree

1. This is the next cen-tury
(Verse 2 see block lyric)
where the u – ni – ver-sal's free,
you can find it a – ny-where, yes the fu – ture's been sold.

Verse 2:
No one here is alone
Satellites in every home
The universal's here
Here for everyone

Every paper that you read
Says tomorrow's your lucky day
Well, here's your lucky day.

He Thought Of Cars

Words & Music by Damon Albarn, Graham Coxon, Alex James & David Rowntree

cow's still red, the young man's dead, gone to heaven in-stead, the eve-ning news says he
(Verse 2 see block lyric)

was con - fused,— the mo - tor-ways will all— merge soon, lot - te - ry win - ner buys the moon, they've

come to save us, the space in - va - ders are here. He thought of

(1, 3.) cars and where, where to drive— them, and

who to drive— them with.— And there,— there was no—

Verse 2:
There's panic at London Heathrow
Everybody wants to go up into the blue
But there's a ten year queue
Colombia is in top gear
It shouldn't snow this time of year
Now America's shot
She's gone and done the lot

He thought of planes and where,
Where to fly to
And who to fly there with
And there, there was no one, no one.

55

It Could Be You

Words & Music by Damon Albarn, Graham Coxon, Alex James & David Rowntree

Verse 2:
The likely lads
Are picking up uglies
Yesterday they were just puppies
Beery slurs now life's a blur.
Telly addicts
You should see them at it
Getting in a panic
Will we be there, Trafalgar Square?

%
Well don't worry
If it's not your lucky number
Because tomorrow there is another
Could be you, could be me.

Ernold Same

Words & Music by Damon Albarn, Graham Coxon, Alex James & David Rowntree

Globe Alone

Words & Music by Damon Albarn, Graham Coxon, Alex James & David Rowntree

1. Who mad-dest one on the M. 1., who has-n't stopped
(Verses 2 & 3 see block lyric)

suck-ing his thumb? Who ve-ry straight and nev-er grins,

who cares what car he's driv-ing in? He is be-cause he saw it on a

com-mer-cial break and if he does-n't get what he wants then he'll

get a head-ache— be-cause he needs it, wants it, al-most loves it.

He's here on his own,— on globe a - lone,— here on his own.—

To Coda ⊕

1.

2.

— On globe a - lone.—

And then he said.

Verse 2:
Who joined health club to glisten
Into hi-fi precision?
Who mobile phone gives him the bone
Who very keen on Sharon Stone?

Verse 3:
Who only eats at the new brasserie
Who only ever gets merry?
Who wouldn't be seen at bedtime
Without putting Calvin Kleins on?

Dan Abnormal

Words & Music by Damon Albarn, Graham Coxon, Alex James & David Rowntree

1. Mea - nie Lea - nie, come— on down,— come and en - ter - tain—
(Verse 2 & 3 see block lyric)

— the town.— It's Fri - day night and we're— all bored,—

2° (Te - le - port   me.)

(Te - le - port   me.)

D.C. al Coda

Dan went to his lo-cal bur - ger bar,   I want Mc - Nor-mal and chips— or I'll blow you to bits,— give us it!

Coda

Dan ab - nor - mal, not nor - mal at—— all,   it's not his—— fault, we——
V.)

Verse 2:
The meanie leanie stays up late
Mopes around, gets in a state
He's the killer in your arcade
Shooting gangstas ready made
'Cause that is where the future's made.

Verse 3:
It's the miseries at half past three
Watching video nasties
He has dirty dreams while he's asleep
Dan's just like you, you and me
He's the meanie leanie.

Yuko and Hiro

Words & Music by Damon Albarn, Graham Coxon, Alex James & David Rowntree

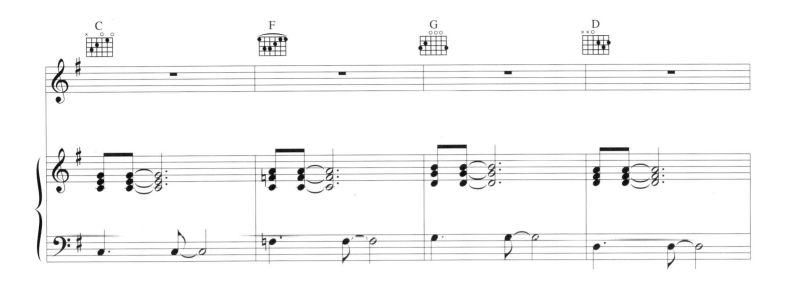

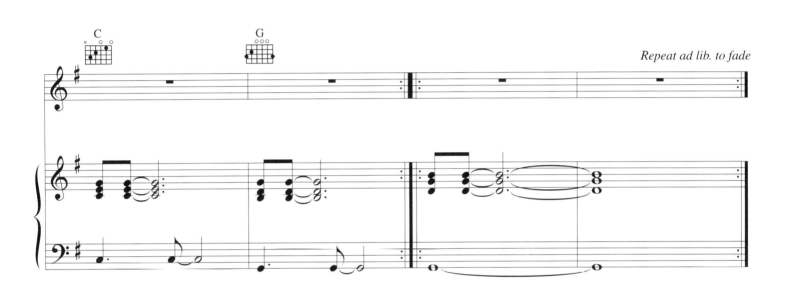

Repeat ad lib. to fade

Verse 2:
I drink in the evenings
It helps with relaxing
I can't sleep without drinking
We drink together
From Monday to Saturday
I go to my workplace
But on Sunday we are together
Yuko and Hiro.

Entertain Me

Words & Music by Damon Albarn, Graham Coxon, Alex James & David Rowntree

1. The

Verse 2:
At his and hers dating
Bored minds agree
Requirements to be stated
Replies awaited
She wants a loose fit
He wants instant whip
He guesstimates her arrival
Will she want it really badly?